Introducing
SQLite for Mobile
Developers

Jesse Feiler

Apress®

Introducing SQLite for Mobile Developers

ISBN-13 (pbk): 978-1-4842-1765-8

ISBN-13 (electronic): 978-1-4842-1766-5

Managing Director: Welmoed Spahr
Lead Editor: Jeffrey Pepper
Technical Reviewers: Aaron Crabtree and Cliff Wootton
Editorial Board: Steve Anglin, Pramila Balan, Louise Corrigan, Jonathan Gennick,
    Robert Hutchinson, Celestin Suresh John, Michelle Lowman, James Markham,
    Susan McDermott, Matthew Moodie, Jeffrey Pepper, Douglas Pundick,
    Ben Renow-Clarke, Gwenan Spearing
Coordinating Editor: Mark Powers
Copy Editor: Lori Jacobs
Compositor: SPi Global
Indexer: SPi Global
Artist: SPi Global

Distributed to the book trade worldwide by Springer Science+Business Media New York, 233 Spring Street, 6th Floor, New York, NY 10013. Phone 1-800-SPRINGER, fax (201) 348-4505, e-mail orders-ny@springer-sbm.com, or visit www.springer.com. Apress Media, LLC is a California LLC and the sole member (owner) is Springer Science + Business Media Finance Inc (SSBM Finance Inc). SSBM Finance Inc. is a Delaware corporation.

For information on translations, please e-mail rights@apress.com, or visit www.apress.com.

Apress and friends of ED books may be purchased in bulk for academic, corporate, or promotional use. eBook versions and licenses are also available for most titles. For more information, reference our Special Bulk Sales–eBook Licensing web page at www.apress.com/bulk-sales.

Any source code or other supplementary materials referenced by the author in this text is available to readers at www.apress.com/9781484217658. For detailed information about how to locate your book's source code, go to www.apress.com/source-code/. Readers can also access source code at SpringerLink in the Supplementary Material section for each chapter.

Contents at a Glance

Contents

About the Author

Jesse Feiler is a developer, consultant, and author specializing in database technologies and location-based apps. He has worked with databases and data management on computers from mainframes to iPhone, iPad, and Apple TV using data management tools from DB2 (IBM) and DMSII (Burroughs) to Enterprise Objects Framework and Core Data, MySQL, Oracle, and, of course, SQLite.

In the early days of the web, he built the page caching mechanism for the Prodigy web browser for Mac using a relational database library similar in some ways to SQLite.

He is the creator of Minutes Machine the meeting management app, as well as Saranac River Trail app a guide to the Trail that includes location-based updates as well as social media tools. His apps are available in the App Store and are published by Champlain Arts Corp (champlainarts.com). As a consultant, he has worked with small businesses and nonprofits on projects such as production control, publishing, marketing and project management usually involving FileMaker and other databases.

His books include:

iOS Programming with Swift for Dummies (Wiley, 2015)

Swift for Dummies (Wiley, 2015)

iOS App Development for Dummies (Wiley, 2014)

iWork for Dummies (Wiley, 2012)

Videos include:

Mixed Language App Development with Objective-C and Swift (O'Reilly, 2015)

iOS Developer's Guide to Views and View Controller (O'Reilly, 2015)

Learning Objective-C Programing (O'Reilly, 2015)

He is heard regularly on WAMC Public Radio for the Northeast's The Roundtable, and is the founder of Friends of Saranac River Trail. A native of Washington DC, he has lived in New York City and currently lives in Plattsburgh NY.

He can be reached at northcountryconsulting.com (consulting) and champlainarts.com (app development).

About the Technical Reviewers

Trained in computer engineering, multimedia, and graphic design, **Aaron Crabtree** has spent the last 15 years working in the industry. Experience has taught Aaron that, in most cases, programmatically creating each piece of an application is necessary for greater flexibility and control. Drop him a line on Twitter: @aaron_crabtree

Cliff Wootton is a former Interactive TV systems architect at BBC News. The "News Loops" service developed there was nominated for a BAFTA and won a Royal Television Society Award for Technical Innovation. An invited speaker on pre-processing for video compression at the Apple WWDC conference. Taught post graduate MA students about real-world computing, multimedia, video compression, metadata and researching the deployment of next generation interactive TV systems based on open standards.

Currently working on R&D projects investigating new Interactive TV technologies, involved with MPEG standards working groups, writing more books on the topic and speaking at conferences when not lecturing on Multimedia at the University of the Arts in London.

Acknowledgments

What I love most about working with databases is putting the pieces of the puzzle together – what a friend of mine used to call "making order out of chaos." When it comes to thinking about SQLite, there are many pieces to put together – everything from the first work on relational databases back in the 1960s to the idea of lightweight code libraries that can fit appropriately onto heavy-duty computers, as well as small battery-powered mobile phones and autonomous satellites designed to explore other worlds far from the relative safety of their home planet.

This book has been made possible, first and foremost, by D. Richard Hipp who began (and continues) the SQLite project starting in 2000. The many people who have added and tested code are too many to thank, but you know who you are.

Closer to home, Jeff Pepper at Apress has been great to work with (again), as has Mark Powers. Together with Carole Jelen at Waterside Productions, they have all made it possible to provide this basic introduction to SQLite.

Introduction

I have worked with databases of many types on many platforms. Despite the fact that almost all of them have been based on the relational model. I've had some excursions into ancient database structures such as IMS (a hierarchical database) and, more recently into unstructured data, but in every case it has been a matter of a basic principle: finding the simplest way to organize data so that it makes sense. (As I often say to clients, "The data doesn't lie." When you lay data out this way, that way, and every which way, I've found that gradually its inherent structure becomes clear – if there is one. If there isn't an inherent structure, what may become clear is some structure no one has ever thought of for the data. And sometimes, the data stubbornly refuses to reveal a structure that we can understand.

This may sound very highfalutin and esoteric, but I do think that our job as database designers ultimately becomes a job of finding patterns. If we cannot find a logically inherent and inevitable pattern, the best choice is to find the best pattern that is usable for the task at hand.

We can't produce these data models without knowing something (a lot, in fact) about the ways to organize data, and, today that comes down to the relational model and the tools of SQL. This process is iterative (woe betide the design team that adopts a partial database model too early), and it relies on flexible tools as well as imagination and constant questioning of everyone working on a project.

SQLite has become a critical component of many data modeling projects because it is so lightweight and flexible. You can put up a SQLite database with basic functionality very quickly. That's where this book comes in. If you have the data and the mission to come up with something that uses the data – website, mobile app, or standalone software product – SQLite can be just what you want.

SQLite runs on many operating systems. With SQLite, you're working with a database that you can move around from one platform to another and one development environment to another. Your prototyping, experimentation, and development can proceed without committing yourself to anything besides the relational model and SQLite. You may move on to other relational tools, and your little SQLite app may turn into a production app for a multitude of devices or for a single many-multi-threaded corporate data center.

This flexibility and very low barrier to entry are two of the features that many people including me find attractive in SQLite.

I hope that you'll find this book useful. There's more information on SQLite at sqlite.org, and there's more information (and downloadable examples from the book) on my website at northcountryconsulting.com.

—Jesse Feiler

■ ■ ■

CHAPTER 1

Getting Up to Speed with Databases and SQLite

Ask people to tell you words they associate with *database* and you'll probably get *big* among the responses. Databases handle large amounts of data, and everyone knows that. How big? It depends whether you count the number of items in a database or the size of the items. The Library of Congress has 160 million items on 858 miles of shelving as of this writing. The catalog, which is based on a database, is available online at www.loc.gov/about/fascinating-facts/. There's no question among people who are interested in databases that the Library of Congress catalog is far from the largest database in the world. (In all likelihood, the largest databases are not visible to the public because they contain classified corporate and governmental information.)

This chapter provides an introduction or reminder about databases today and how they are used. If you've used databases in the past, much has changed, and if you haven't used them much in the past, this chapter will give you a quick overview.

Moving Beyond *Big*

Beyond *big*, you should start thinking about databases as being *structured* and *organized*. In fact, as a mobile developer, the structured and organized aspects of databases are much more important than their size. From the earliest days of the Web in the early 1990s, web browsers have used databases to store and organize their data. What data, you may wonder? How do you think your browser is able to store your passwords for the web sites you visit? How do you think browsers store web pages in a cache so that they can be retrieved without a new network access when possible? And what about your preferences for default font sizes? Or the download folder for files you can change when you feel like it, and even, on many browsers, restrictions on certain users or types of users? These are just simple examples, but the principles apply even to the largest (and smallest) databases today.

Databases Are Structured and Organized

All those examples can be implemented with a database because all those items need to be structured and organized. Some of the items can turn into large amounts of data (particularly a browser history if you don't choose an option to clear out the old information occasionally—another option that can be stored in a preference database), but some of the preferences listed are very small amounts of data: even with a fully modified file name for your download folder, 128 characters is enough to store that data element. Furthermore, most browsers store the name of your preferred download folder, but they don't store the history of download folders (last week's preferred download folder, the folder you used last month, etc.).

In thinking about databases, "big" is often relevant, but very frequently it's misleading. It is structure and organization that matter most.

And they matter a great deal to a mobile developer.

Precisely because mobile devices need to function in a world of constrained resources (e.g., limited storage space and battery power), structuring and organizing the data that is stored is particularly important. Built into a data management system are various optimizations that matter to databases large and small. For example, many databases can store character or string data. Such data is typically quite variable. Even if a database designer specifies that a text field can contain 50, 500, or 50,000 characters, behind the scenes trailing blanks are often discarded. The user (and even the developer) may never know this, but it makes the entire database function more efficiently. (Features like this function behind the scenes and they can be accessed and turned on or off by the database designer in many cases.)

Databases Are Smart

Being able to optimize storage to work with the presence or absence of characters in a text field is a powerful behind-the-scenes tool, but databases have intelligence built into them.

In most database engines today, the designer can specify many attributes of a field such as the following:

- *Name*. A name that is used internally is often quite different from the name that appears in the user interface.

- *Type*. You can specify that a certain database field must be an integer or a string or any other type that the database supports.

- *Optionality*. Some fields are optional, and you can specify that when you set up a database. (Many people have a car with a license number; many other people do not own cars.)

- *Default values*. A database can be set to provide a default value—either a simple value or a calculated value based on other data in the database.

- *Cardinality*. Sometimes, there are multiple values for part of the database. (To continue the example, some people have no car, other people own a car, and others own several cars. Furthermore, some people own a car and a bike . . . you get the idea.)

- *Value ranges*. When the database designer specifies the database structure, a range of values for each field can be set. A driver's license identifier that consists of characters other than letters and numbers (depending on the locality) may not be allowed.

- *Value relationships*. You can move beyond value ranges in designing a database. You can create combinations of attributes and values so that, for example, a database can enforce a rule that an employee may be married (to one person or no one), but if the employee is married, the spouse's employer cannot be the same as the employee's employee. These restrictions in the database reflect policies, but there well may be exceptions (a supervisor's approval), and the database can be designed to support a case like that.

These are just a few of the ways in which a database can be set up to enforce logical rules.

Perhaps at this point you're tempted to say, "But I can do each of those things with a line or two of code." That's absolutely true. But there are a couple of points to bear in mind.

Writing Code Is Just the Beginning

You can write the code to implement any of those conditions, but that's just the start. Over time, conditions change, users have suggestions, and the Power That Be (whoever that (or "they") may be in your life) decides to change the rules for employment, cars, the conditions that apply to license plate numbers, or any other things that strike his or her fancy.

The code that took only a few lines of code and a couple of minutes to write needs to be rewritten. And, although there is no clear research on the matter, it seems that these changes take place at the last minute before a product (or version) launch and they must be done immediately.

Parlez-vous Python? Sprechen Sie Scala?

The line or two that implement the rules for one of the data conditions may have been written by someone who's no longer around. Even if you wrote them, time may have passed and you may not remember exactly what you were trying to implement (yes, commenting your code is a desirable feature, but life happens . . .)

Those few lines of code may have been modeled on some code from a friend that does exactly (or almost) what you want. Maintaining even the best-written code is a challenge for everyone involved from the first author to the updater to the manager and—eventually the user or manager who asks for "just a little tweak."

3

Relational Databases and SQL to the Rescue

Today, databases are remarkably standardized in their structure—perhaps more so than almost any other concept in the world of information technology. The idea of a relational database was first proposed in 1970 by Edgar Codd, of IBM's San Jose Research Laboratory, and his proposal has become the basis for modern database implementations (see article titled "*A Relational Model of Data for Large Shared Data Banks," Communications of the ACM, 13(6), 377–387 (June 1970)*).

In 1974, Donald D. Chamberlin and Raymond F. Boyce (also from IBM) wrote a paper titled "SEQUEL: A Structured English Query Language" for the ACM (Association for Computing Machinery) SIGFIDET Workshop on Data Description, Access and Control.

The relational model (proposed by Codd), together with SQL, has become the basis for modern database implementations. Books by C. J. Date and others together with Codd's original work on the relational model remain the cornerstones of relational database theory today.

■ **Note**　The name SQL is derived from SEQUEL which turned out to be a trademark of the Hawker Siddeley aircraft company. Today, many people suggest that SQL is not an abbreviation or acronym but is a name in and of itself. Others suggest that SQL is an acronym for structured query language.

The basic concepts of SQL are few. You can visualize them by thinking of a spreadsheet with its rows and columns. (You can also conceptualize them using mathematical set theory and other concepts, but spreadsheets are easier for many people to think about today.)

Following are the basic SQL concepts:

- *Table*. A table is much like a simple spreadsheet with rows and columns. (It's not like a complex spreadsheet that may include several tables. For this discussion, think simple—just rows and columns in a single table.) A table is sometimes referred to as a *relation*, but more often *table* is used.

- *Column*. A column represents a single data element such as "address" or "name." In the database world, a column may be called a *field*. In the world of programming, a column may be called an *attribute* or *property*.

- *Row*. A row represents single observations or set of values with one for each column. Thus, a row in this imaginary simple spreadsheet might represent a person's data. In the database world, a row may be called a *record* or *tuple*.

To retrieve data from a relational database table, you run a *query*. A query is a set of logical instructions that manipulate a given table in such a way as to retrieve the data that you want. The result of a query is another table. The resulting table may be empty (if no data satisfies the query), it may be some or all of the data in the table, and, in some complex queries, it may be larger than the basic table. The results of a query are sometimes called a *view* or a *result set*.

These concepts and terms apply to most databases today regardless of the language in which they are implemented and, perhaps more important, regardless of the database engine or database management system (DBMS) in which they are implemented. Furthermore, databases are sometimes implemented as part of frameworks and languages. Thus, in PHP, you can use PDO (PHP Data Objects) starting with PHP 5.1 to access SQLite. For iOS, you can use the Core Data framework to work with SQLite and other data managers. In these cases as well as others, the idea has been to abstract as much as possible into a framework or other wrapper so that switching databases does not require massive rewrites of code.

SQLite implements most of the SQL standard. The exceptions are listed here `https://sqlite.org/omitted.html`.

Looking Inside a Relational Table and Query

For the remainder of this chapter and several that follow, we are going to use a simple example to learn how to create SQLtables and queries. Table 1-1 shows a simple table that can be used to demonstrate the basic concepts of SQL, queries, and relational tables. It shows some data for a few people and their country of origin. The names of the columns (fields) are PK, Name, and Origin. The values of Name are Cecelia, Leif, and Charlotte; the values for Origin are Australia, Iceland, and United States.

Table 1-1. *SimpleTable*

PK	Name	Origin
1	Cecelia	Australia
2	Leif	Iceland
3	Charlotte	United States

■ **Note**   In a relational database, the columns have names, but rows are not named. In the simple table shown in Table 1-1, the first column (named PK) has three values: 1, 2, and 3. These values happen to correspond to the row numbers, but the sample would work just as well if they were named Chair, Tree, and 15.

You can retrieve data from a table by using a query. As noted previously, the result of a query is a table—perhaps an empty one, perhaps some of the data of the original table, and, in some cases, more data than in the original table. This section shows some typical basic queries. In later chapters, you'll see more about queries as well as details about how to structure them. For now, this is just a taste of what queries can be and do.

Basic Query Structure

In their simplest form, queries consist of three sections.

■ **Note**   The code shown in this section is SQL code. By convention, reserved words in SQL are shown in CAPITAL LETTERS although in most implementations, SQL is case-insensitive.

SQL Action: SELECT

There are a number of verbs in SQL, but SELECT is used to select data from a table. Commands start with that word.

SQL Data to Select: List of Column Names

You can start to form a SELECT statement by listing the names of the columns you want to select. Thus, to retrieve data from the Name column, you would start the SELECT statement with

```
SELECT Name
```

To select data from several columns, you can specify a comma-delimited list as in the following case:

```
SELECT Name, Origin
```

You can select all columns with an asterisk as in

```
SELECT *
```

SQL Data Source: Table Name

You can specify the data source using a clause beginning with FROM. Following is an example:

```
SELECT Name FROM SimpleTable
```

SQL Condition: WHERE

You can specify the condition you want to use for selecting data with a clause that begins with WHERE. For example, you could use that first column (PK) to select a single row.

```
SELECT Name FROM SimpleTable WHERE PK = 2
```

You can also form a condition that is more complex:

```
SELECT Name FROM SimpletTable WHERE PK < 3
```

Looking at Other Query Choices

These are the simplest possible examples: more complex ones will be shown throughout the book, but the basic pattern will remain as follows:

```
SELECT this FROM table WHERE condition
```

You can use several tables as your data source. Thus, if you have names and origins as shown in Table 1-1 in a single table, you could have another table with each person's birthday. You could create a single SELECT statement to retrieve both the name and birthday for anyone; to do so you would have to use two tables. (Don't worry, this is an example you'll see in Chapter 4.)

As noted previously, the result of a SELECT query is itself a table. Thus, you can write a SELECT query that executes a SELECT statement to create a table and then selects data from that resulting table.

With this brief overview of relational databases and SQL, it's time to move on to SQLite itself.

CHAPTER 2

■ ■ ■

Understanding What SQLite Is

Chapter 1 provided an overview of relational databases and SQL that applies to most modern databases regardless of the environment in which you find them (Oracle, MySQL, Microsoft SQL Server, or others). That generality is important because SQLite is part of that picture. In this chapter, however, the focus is just on SQLite and the features of SQLite that you may or may not find in other database environments. Whereas a lot of Chapter 1 may be familiar to long-time database users, much of this chapter may not be because even if it is not SQLite-only, many of the features described in this chapter are not present in other database environments. (To be quite fair, many features of other database environments are not found in SQLite.)

Putting a Database in Perspective

A relational database typically lives inside some kind of containing object. Often, the container is a *database management system* (DBMS). (You may sometimes see references to a relational database management system (RDBMS). For most purposes in today's world, most DBMSs are RDBMSs.)

A database management system such as Oracle provides functionality that goes beyond the database itself, such as user interfaces or developer interfaces; diagnostic, debugging, and maintenance tools; and even sophisticated data display functionality.

In some cases, a database is part of a language, object-oriented class, or framework that, itself, may or may not be a DBMS. For example, PHP has a database class just as does the Android SDK (Yes, one is a language and one is an operating system, but each can provide an object-oriented database class.) You'll find more about these classes in Chapters 6 and 7.

On the other hand, Cocoa and Cocoa Touch provide a Core Data framework for both iOS and Mac. I describe Core Data later in Chapters 8 and 9.

For most of this book, the focus is on SQLite itself, but beginning with Chapter 6, you'll see how to access it when it is inside a DBMS, class, or framework.

Defining SQLite

SQLite is a software library written in C. It was developed by D. Richard Hipp in 2000 originally as part of a contract with the U.S. Navy that was implemented by General Dynamics. Today, it consists of some 184,000 lines of code.

SQLite is in the public domain, so it can be used by anyone. Further details and links to download the source code are available at sqlite.org.

You can compile the source code into a library that, in turn, you can use in an application program. Although you may find references to SQLite as a DBMS, it is, strictly speaking, just this library. The container in which that library is compiled (a class, a framework, or a full-fledged DBMS) provides the larger DBMS functionalities.

IS SQLITE A DBMS?

In some ways, this only matters if that question can be answered in a way that influences the way you design or implement your SQLite-based project. However, if you track down references to SQLite, you'll see that it is usually referred to (correctly) as a library or as a database engine.

The code has been designed from the beginning to be compact and reusable (that reference to its origin with the U.S. Navy is relevant here—when you're on a ship at sea, every resource is limited, including power, space, and weight. Furthermore, in modern ships, technological components must function together even if their origins are with multiple vendors. That's the SQLite environment.

Whether you are worried about the limited resources on a ship, on a mobile device running an operating system such as Android or iOS, or on a small mobile device such as a programmable beacon . . . or even the limited resources on a supercomputer ("limited" is always relative), SQLite is a good choice in many cases.

The following sections highlight some of the major features of SQLite that implement this mandate and that are important to you as you use it in whatever container you choose (DBMS, class, framework, or basic library). These features are important to you as you undertake a SQLite-based project for a mobile device.

The features discussed in this section actually all revolve around the fact that SQLite is a library that is designed to be used by a single user to handle database functionality. (Before you throw up your hands, read on to see how SQLite can function very well in a multiuser and multiprocess environment.) The following are the features to consider:

- SQLite is designed for a single user

- SQLite is self-contained

- SQLite supports transactions and is ACID-compliant

■ **Note** You can find more details on these topics at sqlite.org.

SQLite Is Designed for a Single User

One of the biggest differences between SQLite and most DBMSs is that SQLite is designed for a single user. Most DBMSs manage multiple users including various security features that allow or block access to specific SQL commands and features. Even more important to many people, a DBMS manages contention for resources so that several users can apparently use the same data concurrently.

Apparently is the key word here because although each user typically thinks that he or she has unique access to the database, in fact, behind the scenes the DBMS manages concurrency so that in some cases, it has locked a record to prevent access to it by a second user while another user is updating it.

Single User Doesn't Mean Single-Thread

SQLite manages concurrency within its own environment. This means that it may have multiple threads running at the same time to perform its own tasks, but those threads are managed within the SQLite environment itself. They do not represent separate users.

Using SQLite with Multiple Users

How can you have multiple users when SQLite is designed for a single user? The answer is simple: you manage multiple users yourself. There are a number of ways of doing this, but in general, what you do is to push the multiuser management onto the app, class, or language into which SQLite is embedded. Apps typically have the ability to communicate with one another (subject to security and platform constraints). Thus, although SQLite is not going to manage the case of User A and User B attempting to modify the same *data* at the same time, your app can do so.

Typical concurrency strategies involve either having a master process that manages the concurrency or having a mechanism whereby multiple independent processes communicate without a master process. You find many examples of multiple independent processes in apps such as Dropbox and in many cloud-based apps. (In the case of Dropbox and cloud-based apps, there may be a process continually running somewhere in the cloud and, perhaps separate processes running on active clients. Whether or not control resides in a central process or is distributed among the clients (and master) varies depending on the specific implementation.)

Thus, SQLite is perfectly capable of functioning in a multiuser world; it just needs to be running inside apps or other processes that themselves implement the multiuser features.

SQLite Is Self-Contained

SQLite is self-contained in two ways.

- The code itself is self-contained ANSI-C code. It makes minimal use of C libraries. In fact, the only ones it uses are

  - `memset()`

  - `memcpy()`

  - `memcmp()`

  - `strcmp()`

  - `malloc()`

  - `free()`

  - `realloc()`

- The data store itself is self-contained, portable, and platform-agnostic.

Self-Contained Code

Self-contained code means that when you include the SQLite library in your project (either directly or through a language, class, or framework), you have everything you need. You don't need to include additional libraries.

You don't have to worry about versions, and, once you have a compiled SQLite library, you can generally reuse it without being dependent on changes in components. (Remember, though, that in most cases SQLite is embedded in a language, class, framework, or DBMS so the container is what you will need to update from time to time.)

Because SQLite is in the public domain, you don't have to worry about licenses or license fees. (You can, however, obtain a license as described on `sqlite.org`. That option is provided for some users who need to demonstrate to their management that they actually have the right to use SQLite.)

Remember that SQLite is often contained within a class, framework, or language that you are using so this feature (which to a large extent makes such containability possible) may not be visible to you.

■ **Note** If you go to `sqlite.org`, you'll find the various download options for the SQLite source code. There are options to download it in sections that are combined (*amalgamated*) in the final build. This is done primarily to accommodate development environments that have trouble handling the full build at one time.

Self-Contained Data

The data store that SQLite uses for a database is designed to be self-contained and cross-platform. This means that you can transfer a SQLite file from one environment to another without problems in most cases. (That caveat is necessary because you may encounter issues in specific configurations, but for many if not most SQLite users, the first step in verifying that a database can be moved is to actually move it—this usually works.)

In its most basic (and original) form, each SQLite database is stored in a single file. The file is readable and writable on any platform (subject to environmental constraints on the file). For example, if you place the file on a read-only disk, you can't write to it with SQLite. (This may sound far-fetched, but such things do happen.)

With the database in a single file, users can see it and move it around if they want. (If they do so, the app that you are building must be able to find the file—perhaps with the user's help.) Users can also delete the database file. Because it is self-contained, that's very simple, and it doesn't corrupt other SQLite databases. Of course, the fact that a user may be able to delete the database means that in your implementation, you may want to hide it or place it in protected places. If you do that, you often take advantage of platform-specific features such as hidden folders, but the SQLite file itself remains an ordinary file that can be moved around and copied to other devices.

Because the database file is self-contained, it contains both the database data and its schema (structure if you're not from the database world). In part because each database is self-contained, SQLite is referred to as *serverless* (there is no separate server process).

The fact that a SQLite database can be stored in a single file leads to a common use of SQLite to implement structure and database functionality inside what appears to the user to be a simple file.

■ **Note**   Although SQLite began with the one-database/one-file structure, it now supports write-ahead logging (WAL) as an option. WAL is a technique that optimizes database performance using multiple files. There is more on WAL in Chapter 4.

SQLite Supports Transactions and Is ACID-Compliant

Transaction in the world of databases has a very specific meaning over and above its regular meaning in English. It refers to a set of steps that are done together (usually in sequence, but not necessarily so). Together, these steps are a transaction, and what's important is that the transaction as a whole either succeeds or fails. If any of the steps fails, the entire transaction fails. As a result of transaction failure, the database is said to be *rolled back* to its condition before the transaction began.

When a database supports transactions, the failure of any part of a transaction means the entire transaction fails and the database is set to whatever it was before the transaction started. All of this happens in an ACID-compliant database such as SQLite. As you saw in Chapter 1, there's a lot of code you don't have to write when you're using a database.

ACID is the standard by which most databases are judged today to determine if they support transactions. ACID is an acronym.

- *Atomicity*. This is the all-or-nothing aspect of a transaction. It succeeds or fails as a whole and can never be partially successful.

- *Consistency*. In processing a transaction, the database will start from a valid state and end in a valid state. In other words, a transaction will not violate database rules such as the optionality of attributes as a result of a transaction, but those rules may be violated during the course of the transaction.

- *Isolation*. This means that transactions can be run sequentially or concurrently. They will not interfere with one another. (Isolation requires that a database implement a method for managing concurrency so the operations can be either sequential or concurrent.)

- *Durability*. This means that, on completion, the transaction persists. In practical terms, this generally means that it is committed to disk.

In SQLite (as in many other implementations of SQL), a transaction consists of a number of SQL statements bracketed by

```
BEGIN TRANSACTION
```

and

```
END TRANSACTION
```

There is more on transactions in Chapter 4. You'll see how to define them and how to specify the point to which a failed transaction is rolled back. In that chapter, you'll also see a larger description of how WAL implements atomicity and durability.

CONCURRENCY AND ACID TRANSACTIONS ON MOBILE DEVICES

You may think that when you're writing for a mobile device such as a phone, there's only a single user and this discussion of transactions and ACID compliance doesn't apply. However, the issues of concurrency apply perhaps even more on mobile devices than in other cases.

The reason why you have to think about transactions and their failures on mobile devices is that many of the most frequent tasks you perform on mobile devices involve network access. As anyone who has tried to carry on a phone conversation in a train that suddenly speeds through a tunnel knows, network availability can suddenly disappear on a mobile device.

CHAPTER 3

■ ■ ■

Using SQLite Basics: Storing and Retrieving Data

SQLite is a lightweight library containing a database engine that lets you use a very large subset of SQL to store and retrieve data. As a user, you are most likely to be familiar with an application interface or the interface of a database management system (DBMS) that provides an interface to the database itself. Behind the scenes, your commands (whether text or graphical) are translated into SQLite syntax.

This chapter shows you the basics of creating a table, adding data to it, and retrieving that data. It's a high-level overview to give you a taste of SQLite. The next chapter will drill down into some options and variations you can use. In this chapter, you'll see both a graphical user interface (GUI) and the sqlite3 command-line interface that are part of SQLite. In subsequent chapters, you'll usually see only the SQLite interface because it includes the SQLite commands. In most graphical editors for SQLite, you have an option to type in the SQLite code directly, so those commands should work for you in either environment.

TERMINOLOGY AND DEFINITIONS

"SQLite" is used in various ways in this book as it is used in other documentation and discussions. Following is a guide to what's what in the world of SQLite:

- *SQLite.* As used in this book, SQLite refers to any version of SQLite. You can find source code and precompiled binaries at sqlite.org. When used alone, it refers to the SQLite project and any of its versions.

- *SQLite 3* is the current version of SQLite as of this writing. Thus, SQLite 3 is the third major release of SQLite. In this book, SQLite 3 refers to that version as opposed to other versions (e.g., SQLite 2).

- *SQLite 3.9.2* is the current release version of SQLite. As with any maintained software products, it is being revised as needed, so the numbering convention of major-minor-build is used. In this book, the specific release (3.9.2) is not referred to because it is subject to change.

- *sqlite3* (no spaces and all lower-case) is a command-line utility to help you build and debug SQLite databases and syntax. You can download it from sqlite.php, but if you have SQLite installed in your operating system (OS) or other environment, sqlite3 is probably there.

As you read various materials about databases and relational databases, you may encounter database management systems (DBMSs) and relational database management systems (RDBMSs). Most databases today are relational databases, and almost all of them are based on SQL. There are other types of databases, but they're not widely used at the moment. A particularly interesting approach to data management today is unstructured data, but that is outside the scope of this book.

Using `sqlite3`

sqlite3 is a command-line utility that is part of SQLite 3 (the sqlite2 version is no longer applicable). It runs on OS X (using Terminal) or as sqlite3.exe, which runs on Windows. It allows you to experiment with SQLite code directly, and it is used in this book as a touchstone for SQLite syntax. (When you use a third-party tool such as a graphical editor, you may encounter slight variations in the syntax such as whether or not a semicolon is required at the end of a statement—it is in SQLite.) You end your sqlite3 session with a .quit or .exit. Note the initial period because both are sqlite3 commands, but no semicolon at the end because they are not SQLite syntax (requiring a semicolon).

Most of the sqlite3 code in this book is shown with the prompt at the beginning of each line so that you can see which commands are multiline commands. Remember that you always need a semicolon at the end of a command—you can place it alone on the last line if you've forgotten to enter it before.

sqlite3 works with a temporary database that it creates for you, or alternatively, you can manage your own databases. These commands are shown here because they are sqlite3 commands and not SQLite syntax.

In the following subsections, we will review the basic sqlite3 commands that you need to use the most. You can find more information about the sqlite3 commands at www.sqlite.org/cli.html.

■ **Note** Commands inside sqlite3 start with a period.

Run `sqlite3` and Let It Create a New Database

Just type

sqlite3

When you are finished, type .*exit* or .quit. Here is a simple sample session.

```
Jesses-Mac-Pro:~ jessefeiler$ sqlite3
SQLite version 3.8.10.2 2015-05-20 18:17:19
Enter ".help" for usage hints.
Connected to a transient in-memory database.
Use ".open FILENAME" to reopen on a persistent database.
sqlite> .exit
```

Create and Name a New sqlite3 Database

The command sqlite3 mydatabase will create a new database called mydatabase.

```
Jesses-Mac-Pro:~ jessefeiler$ sqlite3 mydatabase
SQLite version 3.8.10.2 2015-05-20 18:17:19
Enter ".help" for usage hints.
sqlite> .quit
```

Delete the Database

By default, the database is created at the root level of the user (as long as that's the directory set in your command-line editor). Therefore, you can delete it from the Finder if you're on OS X. Just go to your root level (i.e., next to folders such as Desktop, Documents, Downloads, Library, Movies, Music, Pictures, Public, and Sites) and delete the database you have just created.

Run sqlite3 and Open an Existing Database

To open an existing database use the .open command. If you want to change your directory in Terminal (or whatever your command-line editor is, use your standard command (it often is cd). In Terminal on OS X, after you type cd, just drag the folder into which you want to place your files into Terminal: it will pick up the path and insert it into your code.

```
Jesses-Mac-Pro:~ jessefeiler$ sqlite3
SQLite version 3.8.10.2 2015-05-20 18:17:19
Enter ".help" for usage hints.
Connected to a transient in-memory database.
Use ".open FILENAME" to reopen on a persistent database.
sqlite> .open testdb
sqlite> .quit
```

Experimenting with SQLite Syntax

The SQLPro for SQLite editor is useful to demonstrate SQLite syntax because, like a number of other SQLite editors, you can use a higher-level interface such as a graphical user interface (GUI) to manipulate your database, but you can also see the underlying SQLite code that is generated. It is that SQLite code with which you'll be working in the rest of this book.

This section lets you explore SQLite syntax, but remember that most of the SQLite code you'll be creating is going to be embedded in an app that you write (or within a framework, DBMS, or library that is included in your app).

There are a number of lightweight SQL editors available on Web (just search for "SQLite editor"). Because sqlite files are cross-platform, you can use these editors to work with any sqlite file that you have (subject, of course, to security constraints implemented by the operating system). In this chapter, SQLPro for SQLite is used as an example of a simple GUI placed on top of SQLite. It is available at www.sqlitepro.com. This will show you how Table 3-1 (shown previously in Chapter 1 and repeated here) is created from a user's point of view.

Table 3-1. *SimpleTable*

PK	Name	Origin
1	Cecelia	Australia
2	Leif	Iceland
3	Charlotte	United States

Because a graphical editor provides you with a view of what you're doing to your database, it may be easier to use than a command-line interface where there is no guidance beyond the command-line prompt. If you prefer to start out with the command line, rest assured that in this chapter you'll see the graphical representation of the table as you create it, but you'll also see the SQLite syntax that is generated at each step.

■ **Note** DBBrowser is another editing tool for SQLite. It is available for Windows, Mac OS X, and Linux at http://sqlitebrowser.org.

SQLite uses a subset of SQL (a very large subset at that). In addition, there are some minor modifications to standard SQL syntax (and, to be quite blunt, just about every DBMS makes some minor modifications of one kind or another). Rest assured, the SQL shown in this chapter applies in almost every environment. If you download a SQL editor from the Web (i.e., a standard SQL editor and not a SQLite editor), you may actually be using syntax that differs very slightly from SQLite.

In particular, the very common MySQL DBMS has several popular editors—many of them free—but you might find a few minor differences. Most people (including me) function quite well without worrying about these distinctions: if they do crop up they're simple to solve. What may be the most important point to remember is that SQLite syntax as it is implemented in SQLite is available at sqlite.org. SQL itself is not a standard in the way the HTML is, and that's why you may encounter these variations.

ABOUT PRIMARY KEYS

Each row in a SQLite table has a rowid—a unique identifier that lets you access that specific row. Often, a unique rowid is created automatically for a table. It may not even be visible to users. Ideally, a primary key is not only unique but also meaningless.

In fact, a meaningless primary key is generally more useful than one with meaning. If the primary key is a person's name, birthday, or address, it can change. Only a totally meaningless value that has no dependency on anything else can successfully serve as a primary key.

That is one of the reasons that database developers often hide their primary keys—or, in the case of SQLite, they let the database take care of it behind the scenes. If you do not want SQLite to do this for you, the check box in SQLPro for SQLite lets you use the behind-the-scenes mechanism. It is exposed in this example in order to use it in demonstrating relationships in Chapter 4.

Exploring Your `sqlite3` Database with a Graphical SQLite Editor

When you first open your graphical SQLite editor, you'll probably see an empty database (or even no database at all). As is the case with any modern app, you may be given the opportunity to reopen the last opened database or to navigate to an existing database.

■ **Tip** Remember than a SQLite database is in its own file usually with a sqlite extension. If you have more than one SQLite database, you have more than one file. (There may be some related files—see "Write-Ahead Logging" in Chapter 4.)

In your database window, you'll usually see a list of the items in your database (if any exist). The main items that you usually care about are

- *Tables* that contain data. You can retrieve the data using a *query*. Queries return tables—they may have no rows or columns and therefore be empty, but they are tables nonetheless.

19

- *Views* are saved queries that, like all queries, produce a table as their result. Thus, a view is not just a saved query: it also can be used much like a table (the result of the query).

- *System tables* are SQLite tables that are created automatically for you within each database. You may think you're creating a new table, and you are, but, in addition, you are updating the *sqlite_master*, which keeps track of each table in the database.

If there are no tables yet—that is the case if you have just created a new database—you'll typically see a list such as the one at the left of Figure 3-1. There are headers for tables and views (none are present as this is a new database). Under the System Tables header, you can see the single *sqlite_master* table, which is present in each SQLite database.

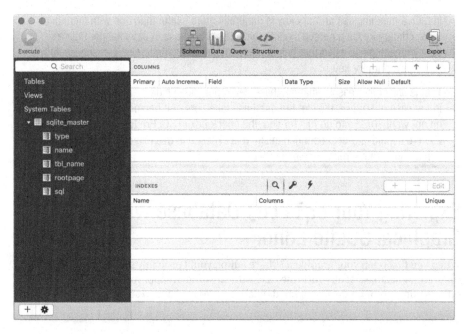

Figure 3-1. *Exploring sqlite_master*

■ **Note** Capitalization doesn't matter in SQLite, but the conventions of using capital letters for SQL syntax and capital names for the names of tables and views is used in this book's text. These are only conventions. Code examples use both upper and lower case. Remember that these are options and conventions, so use what you prefer. If you are working on several projects, you may encounter a variety of styles and conventions. Some people (including me) are in the habit of posting a large sheet of paper on the wall with the conventions for current projects.

If you open sqlite_master, you can see the columns in that table as shown at the left of Figure 3-1. Here they are.

- *type* is TABLE in the case of tables. (Other values will be discussed as they are encountered.)

- *name* is the table name.

- *tbl_name* is a short table name but may be the same as name.

- *rootpage* is used to identify the location in the database where the table is found. You don't often need to refer to this.

- *sql* is the sql code that is used to create the item. It will be updated with modifications so that it is the code to be used to create the item as it is currently configured (not as it was originally configured).

Creating a Table

Here are ways to create a table with a graphical SQLite editor or with the command-line and sqlite3.

Using a Graphical SQLite Editor

At the bottom of the list of tables shown in Figure 3-1 (and near to it in other editors), you'll find a + that lets you add another table to the list. Figure 3-2 shows the result of clicking +.

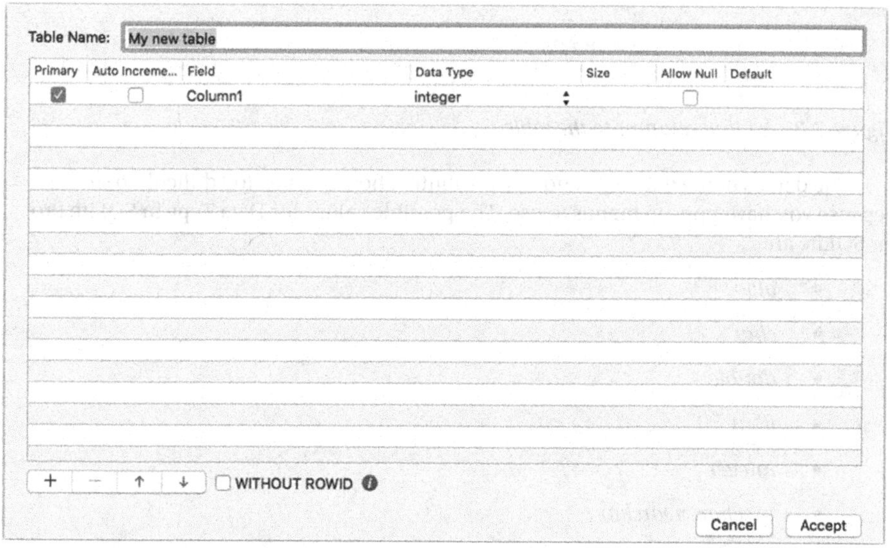

Table Name:	My new table						
Primary	Auto Increme...	Field	Data Type		Size	Allow Null	Default
☑	☐	Column1	integer	↕		☐	

+	−	↑	↓	☐ WITHOUT ROWID ⓘ

Cancel   Accept

Figure 3-2. *Starting to create a new table*

You see a form into which you can type your table name. A single column is placed in the window. The first thing you usually do is rename both the table and the first column.

Creating Table Columns

You can use + to create additional columns. In this case, you know what the table should look like (you've seen it in Table 3-1), so it's not difficult to set up the columns in Figure 3-3.

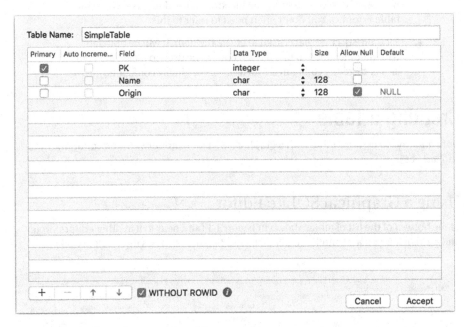

Figure 3-3. *Adding columns to the table*

The details of the data type and size attributes should not be too difficult to set because you have pop-up menus to use. The possible values for Data Type in SQLite Pro for SQLite are

- *blob*
- *char*
- *double*
- *float*
- *integer*
- *varchar, nvarchar*
- *text*

These have the same meanings they have in most languages, but in SQLite, the types are relatively unimportant because SQLite is not strongly typed. It actually uses five basic storage classes.

- NULL
- INTEGER
- REAL
- TEXT
- BLOB

These storage classes are useful in the implementation of SQLite. As noted in the documentation at http://sqlite.org/datatype3.html

Any column in a SQLite version 3 database, except an INTEGER PRIMARY KEY column, may be used to store a value of any storage class.

This doesn't mean that you should ignore typing. In fact, when SQLite is embedded in a framework, DBMS, or language, stricter typing may well be enforced. However, it is the framework, DBMS, or language that enforces that typing.

NULL values are represented by a special code internally that represents nonexistent—NULL. This is far preferable to using an actual value (typically 0 or -1) to represent missing data. As soon as you provide any value for missing data, you run the risk of accidentally using that missing-data value as a real data value. (Ask anyone who worked on the Year 2000 problem what the consequences of this are.) When NULL is not an acceptable value, this means that the relevant column must have some value or other. It can't be totally empty.

In the table as shown in Figure 3-3, *PK* and *Name* cannot be NULL, but *Origin* can be blank.

■ **Note**   A non-null text field must have a value, but it is perfectly acceptable to give it a value of an empty string—that is, a string of zero characters surrounded by quotation marks as in "".

When you have finished specifying your table name and its columns, you click Accept (or whatever your editor calls its button), and the table is created. Remember that inside *sqlite_master* you have a field called *sql* for each table. The field contains the code that generates the table (not its data). You can see that code in SQLPro for SQLite by clicking the Structure button at the top of Figure 3-4.

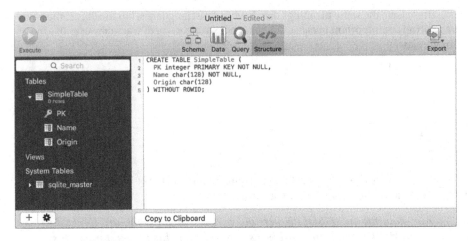

Figure 3-4. *Looking at the SQL code to generate the table*

Using SQLite3

Here's the syntax for `sqlite3`. Note that this syntax creates both the table and its columns. The `ALTER TABLE` command lets you come back later to modify the table's columns.

```
sqlite> CREATE TABLE "SimpleTable" (
   ...>    PK integer PRIMARY KEY NOT NULL,
   ...>    Name char(128) NOT NULL,
   ...>    Origin char(128)
   ...> )WITHOUT ROWID;
```

Inserting Data into a Table

As in the previous section, you'll see how to do this with a GUI as well as with the command line.

Using a Graphical User Interface

In SQLPro for SQLite, the Data button at the top of the window shown in Figure 3-5 lets you add more rows to the column. You can type in the data that you want. Figure 3-5 shows three new rows created, but the only data typed in is located in the first row. You'll notice that the PK primary key is automatically filled in, even in the third row: SQLite has taken care of this because it is the primary key.

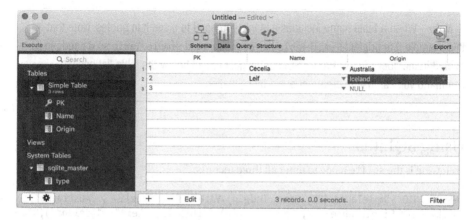

Figure 3-5. *Entering data graphically*

If you want to enter data with a query (here is how you would do it from a command-line interface), you can enter it using the Query button as shown in Figure 3-6.

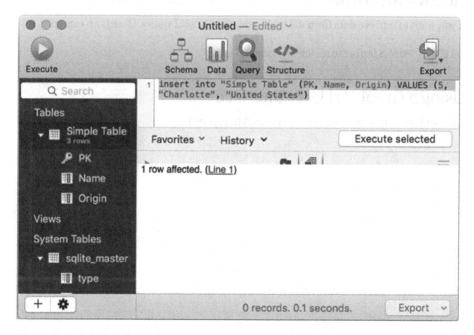

Figure 3-6. *Entering data with a query*

■ **Note** When a table name includes a blank, you need to place it in quotes. Note that in this example, the original SimpleTable has been renamed Simple Table so it needs to be quoted in the query. In SQLPro for SQLite, the gear wheel below the table list has a Rename command you can use to create or avoid this situation.

Using SQLite3

Following is the sqlite3code to enter all three records:

```
INSERT INTO SimpleTable (PK, Name, Origin) VALUES (1, "Cecelia", "Australia");
INSERT INTO SimpleTable (PK, Name, Origin) VALUES (2, "Leif", "Iceland");
sqlite> INSERT INTO SimpleTable (PK, Name, Origin) VALUES (5, "Charlotte",
"United States");
```

Retrieving Data

If you want to retrieve data from the table, you use a SELECT query. Here is an example:

```
SELECT * FROM SimpleTable WHERE Name = "Leif"
```

Using a Graphical User Interface

You can type it into the Query pane as shown in Figure 3-7.

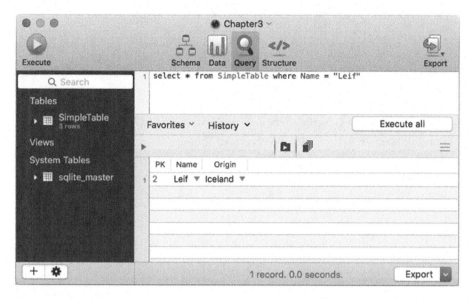

Figure 3-7. *Selecting data with a query*

Using sqlite3

Here's the code in sqlite3. Note how the data is formatted on return with vertical lines between the columns.

```
sqlite> SELECT * FROM SimpleTable WHERE Name = "Leif";
2|Leif|Iceland
sqlite>
```

Deleting Data

If you are playing around with data, you may wind up with data you don't want. In particular, you may be encountering errors because the PK field must be unique so you can't re-enter data you've already entered.

Here's how to delete a row with PK value 1.

```
DELETE FROM SimpleTable WHERE PK = 1;
```

Summary

This chapter has shown you the basics of creating a table, inserting data into it, and then retrieving it. Remember that these are only the basics: in later chapters, you'll see more features of SQLite, but, throughout, the same basic SQLite commands you've seen in this chapter will recur with variations and options. (As a reminder, those commands are CREATE, INSERT, and SELECT.)

CHAPTER 4

■ ■ ■

Working with the Relational Model and SQLite

You've seen how to create a table, add rows to it, insert data into it, and then retrieve the data. Granted, there's not much data involved so far, but these are the basics of database management. Along the way you've seen that SQLite (like many other libraries and data managers) is typically embedded in a framework, language, class, or database management system (DBMS). As noted, today, most DBMSs are relational database management systems (RDBMSs). They are based on the relational model first proposed in 1970 by E. F. Codd, and they typically use SQL or a derivative (like SQLite!) to create, manage, and query the relational database.

You've seen how to use one of the many graphical editors for SQLite (you can find them on the Web searching for "SQLite editor" and perhaps including your operating system in the search). You've also seen how to use basic SQLite syntax directly to create tables and work with their data. This chapter adds another tool to the mix: sqlite3 which is a command-line tool distributed as part of SQLite.

■ **Note**   Most databases today use the relational model, so DBMS and RDBMS are more or less interchangeable terms. This chapter lets you see what is *not* interchangeable: it is only about relational databases (like SQLite). A relational database is a database in which two tables can be *related* to one another. It is the *tables* that are related, and the relationship is created based on *data* in each of the related tables. Thus, although in most of this book *DBMS* is used, in this chapter, because the topic is relational data, we use the term *RDBMS*. Relationships connect two tables, so in order to talk about relationships we need to start with two tables.

Relationships can become very complex (and very powerful) as they are built. For that reason, some people shy away from them, but there is no reason to be concerned. This chapter provides an overview of how relationships work, why you should use them, and how easy it is to create them. Relationships usually involve two or more tables, so this chapter begins by showing you how to create two tables that are logically related. Then you'll see how to use SQLite to actually relate them. (A relationship can actually be created from a single table back to itself. That is called a *self-join*.)

Building the Users Table

Consider the case of keeping score in a multiuser game. You can build on the basics from Chapter 3 to create a table like SimpleTable. In this case, the table is for users. From a data management point of view, there's little difference between a table with names and birthplaces and a table with names and e-mail addresses. (The main difference is that the second table will be more useful in tracking game scores, which is what this example is all about.)

There's another difference that you'll see when you look at the table as shown in Table 4-1 and compare it to SimpleTable (Table 3-1 in Chapter 3). The explicit primary key (column PK) is missing. This table uses the SQLite built-in mechanism for creating a primary key with a unique value for each row. Keep that thought in mind, because we'll return to it shortly.

Table 4-1. *Users Table*

Name	E-mail
Rex	rex@champlainarts.com
Anni	anni@champlainarts.com
Toby	toby@champlainarts.com

■ **Note**   As noted previously, capitalization doesn't matter in SQLite except within parentheses. By convention, SQL keywords are capitalized. In this book, names of tables and columns are typically capitalized in the text; in the sample code they may or may not be to reinforce the fact that it doesn't matter to SQLite. In practice, it's a very good idea to settle on a convention to use. That's because many languages today do recognize the difference between upper- and lowercase letters. Thus, when you switch between writing SQLite code where UseR and user and USER are the same to Swift, Objective-C, Python, C, and others where case matters, you may inadvertently introduce errors for yourself or others by not adhering to a standard. (In addition, standard rules for naming and capitalization make your code easier to read and maintain in the future.)

This is a good start, and you have already seen the code to create such a table in Chapter 3. With the revised column names and data, here's how you can create and populate the table.

```
sqlite> create table users (
   ...> Name char (128) not null,
   ...> email char (128)
   ...> );
```

```
sqlite> insert into users (Name, email) VALUES ("Rex", "rex@champlainarts.com");
sqlite> insert into users (Name, email) VALUES ("Anni", "anni@champlainarts.com");
sqlite> insert into users (Name, email) VALUES ("Toby", "toby@champlainarts.com");

sqlite> select * from users;
Rex|rex@champlainarts.com
Anni|anni@champlainarts.com
Toby|toby@champlainarts.com

sqlite>
```

Now you need the related table which will keep track of scores.

Building the Scores Table

Building the Scores table is basically the same code. For the sake of simplicity, you can let each user start with a score of zero. With that assumption, here is the code.

```
sqlite> create table scores (
   ...> Name char(128),
   ...> score integer
   ...> );

sqlite> insert into scores (name, score) VALUES ("Rex", 0);
sqlite> insert into scores (name, score) VALUES ("Anni", 0);
sqlite> insert into scores (name, score) VALUES ("Toby", 0);

sqlite> select * from scores;
Rex|0
Anni|0
Toby|0

sqlite>
```

Table 4-2 shows the data in Scores at this point.

You can retrieve the data with syntax you've used previously. To get a name and e-mail address from Users, use the following code:

Table 4-2. Scores Table

Name	Score
Rex	0
Anni	0
Toby	0

```
sqlite> select name, email from users where name = "Anni";
Anni|anni@champlainarts.com

sqlite>
```

You get the score from Scores in a similar way;

```
sqlite> select name, score from scores where name = "Anni";
Anni|0

sqlite>
```

Relating the Tables

You need to have a way to refer to two tables in a single SELECT statement (that's where aliases come into play). You also need to actually implement the relationship, and that's where primary keys come into play again. This section covers both topics.

Using Aliases to Identify Multiple Tables in a SELECT Statement

The challenge is to tables and aliases together. You need to select the data for Anni, but there's a problem here: Both Scores and Users have columns called Name. If you use a condition such as where name = "Anni", SQLite won't know which Name column you mean. You can distinguish between those two columns by identifying them in your SELECT statement. It doesn't matter how you identify them, so you could write the following:

```
select a.name, email, score from users a, scores b
  where a.name = "Anni" and b.name = "Anni";
```

You qualify each table with an *alias*. In the *FROM* clause, the alias follows the table name, and in the *SELECT* and *WHERE* clauses, the alias precedes the table name and is separated from it by a period. Thus in the *SELECT* command and *WHERE* clause, you get

```
select a.name
where a.name = "Anni"
```

and in the *FROM* clause you get

```
FROM users a
```

Although you can use anything, you want as the alias; it can make your code easier to read if you use the actual name or an abbreviation for it as in the following:

```
select users.name, email, score from users, scores where users.name =
"Anni" and scores.name = "Anni";
```

Names that are unambiguous (they only occur in one table) don't need aliases.

This structure is very fragile as you will recognize if you've done much work with data and databases. Everything relies on the names being the same in both tables. If there's a misspelling anywhere the data won't match. And even without typos, what happens if a name changes (this happens for a variety of real-world reasons). You could wind up with a handful of Scores records that use the earlier name and another group of records that use the later name.

Before moving on to explore this issue, it's worthwhile to take a look at what's already been done by SQLite behind the scenes: it will help you solve the problems that are unfolding as names change.

Using the rowid Primary Key

In Chapter 3, primary keys that uniquely identify each row in a table were discussed. They're very useful in retrieving data, particularly in cases where the data itself may be incorrect or may have changed from what you think it is, due to revisions or other circumstances. If you don't specify a primary key, SQLite has gone ahead and created a unique key for each row in each table. It's called *rowid*, and you can see it in any table for which you have not provided a primary key. With the Users table shown in this section, you can access the primary keys with the following code:

```
sqlite> select name, rowid from users;
Rex|1
Anni|2
Toby|3

sqlite>
```

This code for *Scores* shows its primary keys.

```
sqlite> select name, rowid from scores;
Rex|1
Anni|2
Toby|3

sqlite>
```

Changing a Name in One Table

In order to change data that's been stored in a row of a table, you use the UPDATE command. Thus, if you want to change Toby to George in the database, you would use syntax like the following:

```
sqlite> UPDATE scores
   ...> SET name = "George"
   ...> WHERE name = 'Toby';
```

You're starting to see how SQL works. The basic clauses such as WHERE and FROM are used over and over again with the same syntax. The only thing that's new in this syntax is the UPDATE command which takes a single table name. Everything else here you have already seen.

If you try to rerun the queries from the previous section, you'll see the data from Users and Scores.

```
sqlite> select * from users;
Rex|rex@champlainarts.com
Anni|anni@champlainarts.com
Toby|toby@champlainarts.com
```

```
sqlite> select * from scores;
Rex|0
Anni|0
George|0
```

```
sqlite>
```

If, in fact, George and Toby are two different people, it's correct that things don't work properly. But if it's the case that Toby has decided to go by his middle name of George now, George and Toby are actually the same person. How do you move all of Toby's data to George?

Retyping or using UPDATE is one way to handle this, but the better way is to use the built-in SQLite primary key as a *foreign key*.

Using a Foreign Key

If you have followed along, you'll be able to see the rowid and name values in both tables using the following syntax. For Users, here is the syntax. Table 4-3 shows the data.

```
sqlite> select rowid, name from users;
1|Rex
2|Anni
3|Toby
```

Table 4-3. *Users Table*

rowid	Name	E-mail
1	Rex	rex@champlainarts.com
2	Anni	anni@champlainarts.com
3	Toby	toby@champlainarts.com

For Scores, this is the syntax:

```
sqlite> select rowid, name from scores;
1|Rex
2|Anni
3|George

sqlite>
```

Table 4-4 shows the scores.

Table 4-4. *Scores Table*

rowid	Name	Score
1	Rex	0
2	Anni	0
3	George	0

The solution is to use a *foreign key*. A foreign key is a value in one table that identifies a row in another table. In this case, you want *rowid* 3 in Users (Toby) to be used to match *rowid* 3 in Scores (George). The names are different (George and Toby), but you want that relationship to work to reflect the fact that they are two different values for the same person.

■ **Note** The fact that *rowid* 3 is the value you want to relate from one file to another is happenstance based on the sequence in which these files have been constructed. Later in this chapter, you'll see how those numbers can have different values, but for now, you will probably see the same values shown here.

The solution is to create a new column—it's usually called *FK* or *Foreign Key* in the database world. Sometimes database designers give it a name that identifies its source such as scorekey or scoreid and userkey or userid. Thus, if you're looking at the Scores table, you could see the primary key or rowid alongside a separate userkey. If you take the values of rowid in Users to be the starting point (since that's probably the first table to be created), you then want to have a matching value for userid in Scores.

To add a column to an existing table, you use the ALTER TABLE command. You specify the name of the table to alter, the name of the column to add, and the type of that column. Here's the syntax to use to create a new column called userid.

```
ALTER TABLE Scores ADD COLUMN userid integer;
```

To see the result of this command, use the .schema command in sqlite3. (Because it's a sqlite3 command, it starts with a period and doesn't require a semicolon at the end. The command takes one parameter which is the name of the table you want to examine. Here's the result if you run it now. You'll see that userid has been added.

```
sqlite> .schema scores
CREATE TABLE scores (Name char(128),
    score integer
    , userid integer);

sqlite>
```

Now you need to enter data for the userid column that you just added to Scores. The userid values in Scores should be the value of the corresponding record in Users. At the moment they're the same, but you'll soon change them.

Here is the syntax to enter data for rowid in Scores. Basically, this is the same way in which you changed the name from Toby to George.

```
sqlite> update scores set userid = 1 where name = 'Rex';
sqlite> update scores set userid = 2 where name = 'Anni';
sqlite> update scores set userid = 3 where name = 'George';
```

For now, just verify that the data in Scores is as shown here (both in SQLite and in Table 4-5).

```
sqlite> select rowid, userid, name, score from Scores;
1|1|Rex|0
2|2|Anni|0
3|3|George|0
sqlite>
```

Table 4-5. Scores Table with userid Added

Rowid	userid	Name	Score
1	1	Rex	0
2	2	Anni	0
3	3	George	0

The names in this table are no longer relevant because the relationship between Scores and Users is based on rowid in Users matching userid in Scores. In SQLite, the ALTER TABLE command does not let you drop a column: The recommended workaround is to drop the table and create a new one (more appropriately in many cases, export the data, import it to a new table, and then drop the old table). So, for now you can just ignore the Name column in Scores. From your perspective, Scores can look like Table 4-6 (even though there's a no-longer-needed column in the actual table).

Table 4-6. *Scores Table with userid Added and Name Ignored*

rowid	userid	Score
1	1	0
2	2	0
3	3	0

Joining the Tables

The simplest way to get the data you want is to use a *WHERE* clause to specify that you want data where users.rowid matches scores.userid. (Remember that SQLite automatically creates users.rowid when you don't provide a primary key, but you must enter the appropriate values of users.rowid into the scores.userid column to make the relationship work.

If you have done that (and if you've followed the steps in this chapter you have done so), the following code will give you what you want:

```
sqlite> select users.name, scores.score from users, scores where users.rowid
= scores.userid;
Rex|0
Anni|0
Toby|0

sqlite>
```

There are several important points to notice here:

- The names come from Users; the Name field in Scores is no longer used. For that reason, even though you still may have George as a name in Scores, userid 3, which started out as Toby, is shown as George (assuming it's the same person with just a name change that is correct).

- Only the matching records are shown. Add some new records to Users or Scores: they won't show up unless the rowid in Users matches the userid in Scores.

- If a record in Scores has no userid, it won't show up.

Summary

You can build on this general structure, just as is, by adding more data. Experiment with combinations of new records, and matching and nonmatching ids for users and scores. Add a Scores record for an existing user so that a person has two records but with the correct names from Names.

In Chapter 5 you'll explore more ways to enhance SELECT statements.

CHAPTER 5

■ ■ ■

Using SQLite Features—
What You Can Do with
SELECT Statements

There's more to SELECT statements than just getting data. In addition to join clauses (discussed briefly in Chapter 4), you can order and group data as well as provide intermediate tables for doing what, in effect, are subselect operations. If you are used to *procedural programming* where you describe each step of a process (do this . . . do that, . . . if this is true do the other thing or else do that thing . . .), you may notice that SQL and relational databases encourage you to think in *declarative programming* ways (get me everything that is X, do something to all the Xs . . .).

When you are working in the world of declarative programming, the more you can put into the declarations the better off you'll be. Translated into English, this means all of the following:

- Instead of writing code to test for valid data, attempt to enforce the validation rules in the database or framework. (The Xcode Core Data model editor takes this to a graphical limit.)

- Rather than looping through each item in a set of data and testing a value to determine which procedural branch to take, get all the Xs and do something to each of them. (In effect, you move the if statement into the SELECT statement.)

This chapter examines a number of SQL clauses that can improve your code. Bear in mind that in effect you are writing some functional code, but in a declarative way, so that you can get to the declarative goal of doing the same thing to every item in a group (or in a SELECT result).

You'll also see how to use variables in SQLite statements. This can dramatically improve your SQLite performance. The concept is implemented in PHP, Android, and Core Data not to mention in many common databases.

Looking at the Test Data

In this chapter, we use some test data in the examples. It's actually some data generated in testing the Score app in Chapter 12. The table that is used is Score, and the values that are used here are rowid (a primary key), userid (a user number and foreign key), and score (a specific score). A given user can have multiple scores, but each user and rowid is unique.

Following is the basic data used:

```
sqlite> select rowid, userid, score from Score;
1|1|10
2|2|20
3|3|30
4|1|99
5|1|99
6|1|9
7|1|99
8|1|99
9|1|17
10|1|31
11|1|23
12|1|50
24|2|16
25|3|8
26|2|99
27|1|3
sqlite>
```

Ordering Data Makes It Easier to Use

The row numbers are in order, but to look at the data in a meaningful way, it makes sense to order it as in the following:

```
sqlite> select rowid, userid, score from Score order by userid;
1|1|10
4|1|99
5|1|99
6|1|9
7|1|99
8|1|99
9|1|17
10|1|31
11|1|23
12|1|50
27|1|3
```

```
2|2|20
24|2|16
26|2|99
3|3|30
25|3|8
sqlite>
```

Grouping Data Can Consolidate It

When you group data, you consolidate it into a single item for each value of the group. If you want to find the maximum value of score, you can use the following code:

```
sqlite> select max (score) from Score;
99
sqlite>
```

■ **Note** In this and the other examples, feel free to refer back to the basic list of data to understand the results.

If you group the data, you can get the maximum value for each userid as in the following:

```
sqlite> select userid, max(score) from Score group by userid;
1|99
2|99
3|30
sqlite>
```

Life isn't just about the biggest and smallest: SQLite helps you find the middle of road (the average). If these scores represent teams rather than users, the winning team based on average scores would be Team 1:

```
sqlite> select userid, avg (score) from Score group by userid;
1|49.0
2|45.0
3|19.0
sqlite>
```

Remember group by the next time you're tempted to write a loop to calculate an average or find the maximum or minimum value. In fact, it you're using a relational database such as SQLite, which supports SQL (even one more basic and less powerful than SQLite), try to catch yourself the next time you start to write a loop to process the results of a query, and ask yourself: "Can I do this inside the query itself?"

41

Using Variables in Queries

In Chapter 6, you'll see how to use SQLite with the PHP data object (PDO). It's a singleton object in your PHP code, but it is definitely an object with its own methods. As you'll see in the next chapter, the process of querying the database consists of using four methods.

- new PDO creates the PDO and connects it to your SQLite database.

- prepare takes as its parameter your SQLite query

- execute performs the query

- $query->fetchAll retrieves the data from the query

There is also a simple query () call that creates and performs the query all at once. Many databases support this type of process—creating a query that can be used and reused as well as creating a query to run once. The reason for exposing the step-by-step query create, prepare, and execute process becomes clear when you realize that you can create variables inside the query.

Thus, the basic query that can be used to get all the names from a user table can be

```
$query = $sqlite->prepare ("select * from users;");
```

The name to retrieve the record for a record with a specific value for name could be

```
$query = $sqlite->prepare ("select * from users where Name = "Rex";");
```

At this point it may seem that it would be easier to use the one-step call which does the "prepare" and "execute" together.

```
$query = sqlite->query ("select * from users where Name = "Rex");
```

However, the power and efficiency of the separate statements become clear if you use a variable. Here's an example. Begin with new PDO and prepare but, inside your query, use a variable such as :name.

```
$sqlite = new PDO('sqlite:sqlitephp.sqlite');
$query = $sqlite->prepare ("select * from users where name = :name;") ;
```

You don't have to use $query right away, but whenever you do decide to use it, fill in the value for :id with code such as the following:

```
$query->bindValue (':name', "Rex");
```

or, if you want to use a variable,

```
$theName = "Rex";
$query->bindValue(':name', $theName);
```

Then execute the query:

```
$query>execute()
```

You can come back later and change the bound value and re-execute the query:

```
$query->bindValue (':name', "Anni");
$query>execute()
```

This process saves some memory and is much more efficient. The query can be prepared with the missing data not yet present so that when you come back to execute it, there's much less work to do.

Summary

In this chapter you've seen some of the extra tweaks you can use with SELECT statements in SQLite. Everything that you can move into the query means a little less code for you to write and debug.

With this background, it's time to move into using SQLite with PHP, Android, and OpenDoc. Each of them does the same thing, but their approaches are a little different. What remains the same is SQLite.

CHAPTER 6

■ ■ ■

Using SQLite with PHP

The basics of SQLite and, indeed, of SQL itself, are simple. It's a repetitive routine of creating tables with a column for each data element in the table. You then add rows to each table with a value for each column. You can retrieve data from a single table with a basic SELECT statement. Join two tables by using a WHERE clause to match a value in one table with a corresponding value in another table (or in the same table in the case of a self-join).

The complexity of SQL and all of its implementations including SQLite comes from combinations of these basic building blocks. In addition, the fact that we are often dealing with very large tables (millions and even billions of rows) are factors that can add complexity to the mix, but the basics are simple.

■ **Note**   There is a SQLite limit of 140 terabytes per database, and that limit would tend to be reached before the number of rows becomes an issue. sqlite.org has a page on limits at www.sqlite.org/limits.html. It notes that these limits are for the most part untested in part due to SQLite developers not having access to hardware capable of managing those amounts of data. If you really are contemplating managing that amount of data, you may want to do a serious analysis of hardware and software solutions, but remember that whatever solution you end up with, SQLite can make a perfect prototyping tool.

SQLite itself is very lightweight: it imposes a minimal burden on users and their devices in many cases. That combination of a simple structure and a lightweight implementation makes SQLite a popular tool for use in web sites. Because it is a single-user implementation, it is often used for a single user's data, but, as noted previously, it also can be used to prototype an implementation of a much larger system using a more powerful SQL implementation of any sort.

Whether you are working with a single-user project or a prototype for something larger, SQLite is a good choice, and it fits nicely with PHP. This chapter provides a brief overview (or refresher) of PHP; it then moves on to show you how the basic tables shown in Chapters 3 and 4 can be implemented on web pages with PHP.

■ **Note** This chapter focuses on the basics of PHP/SQLite integration. For an example of how they can be used on a series of web pages, see Chapter 11. In order to test the code in this chapter, you will need a basic text editor—preferably one such as BBEdit, which highlights syntax for you so you can spot minor typos easily. You also need a server to which you can upload your PHP files as well as a SQLite database. If you are maintaining a web site, you have access to such a server in order to post your HTML pages. It may or may not have PHP installed. Most servers do, but for security reasons some limit access. If you have any difficulties, check with your server administrator.

DEFINING "SINGLE USER" FOR PHP

SQLite is designed for a single user. It is often used together with PHP to implement a website. Does that mean that your PHP/SQLite web site is designed for a single user?

The answer is "yes," but the details may surprise you. When you use PHP in a web page, there is a single user—it is the web server. Depending on your app, SQLite may or may not be a good choice (it almost always is a good choice for prototyping and testing). Static databases work well most of the time if they are not enormous. Apps that need to update a database can quickly run into trouble if you use SQLite and there are more than a handful of users (it also depends on how frequently your users are updating the data).

Putting PHP and SQLite Together: The Basics

PHP is perhaps the most widely used server-side programming language. Strictly speaking, it is a scripting language which means that it is interpreted at runtime (in practical terms, that usually means web page load time). The output from the PHP script is typically a web page in this scenario. As the PHP script is running, it can do a wide variety of things including communicating with other processes and devices, and in the SQLite context, it can communicate with a SQLite database that resides on the web server.

Verifying PHP in Your Environment

Start by verifying that you have PHP installed on your server and that you can access it. (If you already are using PHP for web sites or other files, you can skip this step.)

Here is the code for a simple PHP-based web page. It simply requests a display of the current PHP status information on the server. If it doesn't work, check with your administrator because you won't be able to experiment with SQLite and PHP if the PHP piece is missing. In addition to PHP, you may also have to verify that SQLite is available on the server, but in many (probably most) cases it is.

■ **Caution**   Unlike SQLite, PHP is case-sensitive, so be careful with your capitalization. This is a good reason for standardizing on case-sensitive names for column names in your SQLite code even though it doesn't matter to SQLite. When you start manipulating the data with PHP, it will matter.

This is the sample code to use to test PHP. The code in boldface is the PHP code inside the HTML code—it is delimited by <?PHP and ?>. It simply calls the phpinfo() function. Place this code in a file on your server. This file should have the php extension (it is usually lower-case, but on many servers the case won't matter). If you name this test.php and upload it to the root of your web site (next to index.html or index.php in most cases) you can access it—including running the embedded PHP code—by going to http://mywebsite/test.php.

```
<!DOCTYPE html>
<html>
<head>
        <title>Chapter6</title>
        <meta name="generator" content="BBEdit 11.1" />
</head>
<body>
<?PHP
  phpinfo();
?>
</body>
</html>
```

Preparing the SQLite Database

You can use almost any of the SQLite commands with PHP, but, in practice, the most common commands you use are those that manage data in a table that already exists. In some environments, it may be an empty table that is populated by your web site as it is visited by users.

Here is the code to prepare the pair of databases used in Chapter 4. They will be used again in this chapter. Several sections are worth paying particular attention to. They are shown in bold.

- In this example, sqlite3 is launched using a database called sqlitephp.sqlite. If it doesn't exist, sqlite3 creates it. Normally, sqlite or db is used as the extension. (If you use your own extension, you may have issues in uploading it to your web site.)

- The Users table is created. Note that the Name column cannot be null—you must have a name. Data already used in Chapter 4 is filled in. (It is shown here as Table 6-1.)

Table 6-1. *Users Table*

rowid	Name	E-mail
1	Rex	rex@champlainarts.com
2	Anni	anni@champlainarts.com
3	Toby	toby@champlainarts.com

- After creating the table and inserting the data, the data is shown with a SELECT statement. Note that the rowid is specifically requested: The typical SELECT * shows all columns except a hidden column such as rowid.

- You need to see the rowid values in order to insert them into Scores. The insert statement inserts the rowid values into Scores so that the relationship can be used. Table 6-2 shows the Scores table.

Table 6-2. *Scores Table*

userid	Score
1	10
2	20
3	30

- Finally, a SELECT statement shows the name and score using data from both Users and Scores that is related using rowid (users) to userid (scores). Table 6-3 shows the data.

Table 6-3. *Related Users and Scores Tables*

Name	Score
Rex	10
Anni	20
Toby	30

The entire sqlite3 code is shown here.

```
Jesses-Mac-Pro:~ jessefeiler$ sqlite3 sqlitephp.sqlite
SQLite version 3.8.10.2 2015-05-20 18:17:19
Enter ".help" for usage hints.

sqlite> create table users (Name char (128) not null, email char (128));

sqlite> insert into users (Name, email) VALUES ("Rex",
"rex@champlainarts.com");
sqlite> insert into users (Name, email) VALUES ("Anni",
"anni@champlainarts.com");
sqlite> insert into users (Name, email) VALUES ("Toby",
"toby@champlainarts.com");

sqlite> select rowid, name from users;
1|Rex
2|Anni
3|Toby

sqlite> create table scores (userid integer, score integer);

sqlite> insert into scores (userid, score) VALUES (1, 10);
sqlite> insert into scores (userid, score) VALUES (2, 20);
sqlite> insert into scores (userid, score) VALUES (3, 30);

sqlite> select name, score from users, scores where userid = users.rowid;
Rex|10
Anni|20
Toby|30

sqlite>
```

Upload your database to your web server. It should be visible on your desktop in the Finder (OS X) or Start (Windows). In this example, it is uploaded to the root of your web site.

PDO VS. OLDER PHP/SQLITE DATABASE CONNECTIONS

There have been two main ways of connecting SQLite to your database. The older one is a procedural style, and the newer one (since that long-ago year of 2005) is object-based. The PDO extension (PHP Data Object) is more robust and a better choice in every case except when you are tasked with modifying old PHP code that accesses SQLite databases in the older style.

If you are leary of using object-oriented programming, rest assured that PDO is indeed object-oriented, but it works very well with standard PHP code. You don't have to convert all of your code to objects and classes: you can use PDO for your SQLite database and, unless you really know what you're looking for, you may not even realize that you're using an object.

PDO is an extension to SQLite, but the extension is built into the current versions; in fact, you need to make an effort to not have it available. It is described in this section. Although you may find sample code in various places on the Web, remember that PDO is now over ten years old, and it's the current version. You may have difficulties opening older SQLite databases with the older style of code. (If you find sqlite_open in code you're looking at, that's the older—non-PDO—style.)

Connecting to Your SQLite Database

There are five steps involved and we will discuss them in detail shortly.

1. **Create a new PDO instance**. It contains the name of the database to which you want to connect.

2. **Create a query**. It typically is placed in a variable called $query, but you can use any name you want. The query is created by calling the prepare method on your PDO instance. If it succeeds, it returns a PDOStatement object.

3. **Execute the query**. You do this by calling the execute method on the query (PDOStatement) that you have just created as in $query->execute(); It returns TRUE or FALSE but it does not return any values to you (yet).

4. **Fetch the results from the executed query**. (Now you have the data.) The data is typically stored in an array variable called $results. You can use $query->fetch(); to fetch the next row of results. You can use $query->fetchAll(); to get an array of all results. Which method you choose is up to you and depends on your specific needs (and how much data you expect to retrieve). By default, the fetched results are in an associative array with elements identified by SQL column names.

5. **Use the results of the query that you prepared, executed, and then fetched.**

Here are the details of each step.

You start with a PHP file that you want to use to access your SQLite with the five steps shown here. If you name this file phpsql.php and upload it to your web site, you can access it with http://mywebsite/phpsql.php. The full file is shown later in this chapter. Here are the relevant components in detail.

1. Create a New PDO Object

Create a new PDO object and place it in a local variable. Often, that variable is named $sqlite, but you can use any name you want. When you create the new PDO object, you must pass in the name of the SQLite file, including any paths relative to the location on the server where your PHP file is. The quoted name starts with the data source name (DSN) sqlite:. This is part of the quoted string that includes the file's location.

Following is an example:

```
$sqlite = new PDO('sqlite:sqlitephp.sqlite');
```

There is another style you can use. It may or may not be clearer for you (and the people who will revise your code in the future). These are interchangeable.

```
$db = 'sqlite:sqlitephp.sqlphpproject';
$sqlite = new PDO($db);
```

■ **Note**   There are other DSN strings including mysql, pgsql (Postgres), msql, sybase, or dblib (SQLServer or Sybase), odbc, ibm (IBM DB2), informix, firebird (Firebird or Interbase).

HANDLE ERRORS PROPERLY

It's a good practice for your users (and for yourself when debugging) to handle errors neatly. The "or die" clause does that in a very basic level. You provide a string that is displayed. In the case of PHP code generating a web page, the quoted string can include HTML formatting as in this example:

```
$sqlite = new PDO('sqlite:sqlitephp.sqlite')
  or die ("<h1>Can't open database</h1>");
```

For debugging purposes you may want to provide a diagnostic message when or die doesn't fail. You can always take these messages out before moving to production but they'll help you follow along with each step to see whether or not it succeeds.

```
echo "<p>Success on PDO</p>";
```

It's better ultimately to use a try/catch block, but or die is more concise and is used to simplify the code in this book.

2. Create and Prepare the Query

You use the same queries that you use directly in an interactive editor like sqlite3 in any other environment. The only difference with PDO is that you create the query in a single step before you use it.

Here is an example of creating a query, storing it in a variable, and catching failures as well as logging successes (the latter only for debugging). Note that you have to use the prepare method on the instance of PDO that you have created — in this case it's $sqlite.

```
$query = $sqlite->prepare ("select Name from users;")
  or die ("<h1>Can't prepare</h1>");
echo "<p>Success on prepare</p>";
```

3. Execute the Query

Now that you have created a query, with the prepare method of your PDO instance, call the execute method on that query to actually run it. As usual, catch errors and, for debugging, print out successes as well. Here is the code. Note in this example that the or die clause doesn't use any specific HTML formatting. That is only to show you that it can be done either way.

```
$query->execute() or die ("Can't execute");
echo "<p>Success on execute</p>";
```

4. Fetch the Results

The execute method returns TRUE or FALSE, but the data isn't available until you fetch it. (If you've used other databases before, you'll recognize this pattern.) You can get all of the rows at once with fetchAll, or you can get each one separately with fetch.

The fetch version gets one row at a time. By default, it returns the next row of the results set as an array indexed by column name as well as by a zero-relative column number reflecting the items in your SQLite SELECT statement. There is also an optional $cursor_offset parameter which lets you jump around in the results set.

The fetchAll version gets all of the data at once as an array. You'll see both fetchAll and fetch in the following step.

5. Use the Results

You loop through the returned array elements in your code. In either case, you echo the result value(s) in your PHP code, combining the returned value with any HTML you want to use. For example, in the fetchAll scenario, you loop through each returned row, placing each row into a local variable (typically called $row, but you can use any name you want).

Here is the relevant fetching and looping code. (It refers to the Users table shown previously in Table 6-1.)

```
$result  = $query->fetchAll() or die ("Can't fetchAll");
echo "Success on fetchAll "; // for debugging
foreach ($result as $row) {
  echo "<p>Name: {$row['Name']}</p>";
}
```

Putting together all of the steps in this chapter you can get a PHP file such as the following. Remember to customize it for your database name and the column name(s) you want to display. The code to customize is shown in bold.

■ **Note**   Customize the HTML for the page you want to create, but also see Chapter 11, which adds more typically used HTML code that works well with SQLite.

```
<html>
  <head>
  </head>
  <body>
<?php

        $sqlite = new PDO('sqlite:sqlitephp.sqlite')
          or die ("<h1>Can't open database</h1>");
        echo "<p>Success on PDO</p>";

        $query = $sqlite->prepare ("select Name from users;")
          or die ("<h1>Can't prepare</h1>");
        echo "<p>Success on prepare</p>";

        $query->execute() or die ("Can't execute");
        echo "<p>Success on execute</p>";

        $result  = $query->fetchAll() or die ("Can't fetchAll");
        echo "Success on fetchAll ";

        foreach ($result as $row) {
          echo "<p>".$row['Name']."</p>";
        }
?>
  </body>
</html>
```

Summary

This chapter shows the basic steps involved in connecting to a SQLite database.

1. Specify the database to use.

2. Create a query to use in retrieving data.

3. Run the query.

4. Fetch data from the query results.

5. Use the results in your code.

These steps apply to SQLite, but they also apply (sometimes with slightly different terminology and definitely different syntax) to the other languages and frameworks you use to retrieve SQLite data. Furthermore, these same basic steps apply to other databases than SQLite. This is the basic paradigm for retrieving data from a database.

The following chapters show you how to use other languages than PHP to make your SQLite database connections.

CHAPTER 7

■ ■ ■

Using SQLite with Android/Java

In part because it's lightweight and in the public domain, SQLite is an obvious choice for many projects where there are constraints on space, power, and cost. For those and other reasons, it's built into a variety of operating systems and is used on many devices.

This chapter shows you some of the key elements of using SQLite with Android. It's built into android.database.sqlite, so it's there for you to use. The basics of using SQLite are the same whether you're using PHP to build a web site (see Chapters 6 and 10) or you're using Core Data on iOS or OS X (see Chapters 8 and 12).

Integrating SQLite with Any Operating System, Framework, or Language

No matter what development platform you're using, integrating SQLite in your app is always the same (and, indeed, this applies to any database).

1. Design your database. This is not a SQLite issue. See the sidebar, "The Critical Database Design Step."

2. Connect your app to the database at runtime.

3. Use the connection to add, delete, insert, or update data.

4. Use the results of the operation in your app. This may consist of refreshing the interface by adding or removing items, or it may consist of working with the data in a new item or anything else you and your users require. This is not a SQLite issue.

THE CRITICAL DATABASE DESIGN STEP

The first step has almost nothing to do with your development environment. Identifying your data, figuring out the relationships and defining validation rules don't require anything more than thinking, discussion, and some sketching of the database. A key part of this step is naming the components (is it "Client" or "User" or "Customer") in such a way that end users and people who develop and maintain the code will understand what's going on.

This is a critical and much-overlooked aspect of the development of any app that relies on data (whether it's a relational database, a key-value store, or a flat file). This book focuses on SQLite, but if you're not familiar with the concepts of data management and the design tools that are available, make certain that you get up to speed at least to a basic level quickly.

There is a sort of progression in the integration of SQLite with PHP, Android/Java, and Core Data for iOS and OS X. With PHP, you are typically working with very visible SQLite code, and, as you will see, it is frequently procedural code for the most part. When you get to Core Data, you'll be working with object-oriented code where the framework and its classes use SQLite code behind the scenes: you will rarely write SQLite code directly, but you're using it all the time. Android and Java strike a middle ground so that the SQLite code is more visible than it is in Core Data, but it's not as visible as it is when you're using PHP.

Although there are object-oriented ways of writing PHP code, by and large you are working in a procedural environment. However, in today's world, the recommended best practice for integrating PHP with a database is to use the PHP data object (PDO) extension. That is an object-oriented class which encapsulates the code that you need to work with for a database. There are versions for SQLite and other major databases so your PDO code is relatively easy to port.

Chapter 6 showed you the coding basics of using SQLite with PHP. Here is the summary of the steps. This is only a summary. In practice, you'll flesh out the foreach loop and you'll probably replace or die with a try/catch block.

```
$sqlite = new PDO('sqlite:sqlitephp.sqlite');

$query = $sqlite->prepare (...SQLite query...);

$query->execute() or die ("Can't execute");

$result = $query->fetchAll() or die ("Can't fetchAll");

foreach ($result as $row) {
    ...work with each result row
}
```

Using Android and SQLite

The Android NotePad example is an excellent example of the integration of SQLite with Android. You can download it from https://android.googlesource.com/platform/development/+/05523fb0b48280a5364908b00768ec71edb847a2/samples/NotePad/src/com/example/android/notepad/NotePadProvider.java.

The NotePadProvider code in that example extends ContentProvider which encapsulates the basic SQLite functionality that you need. This is the sort of code that you'll need in your own app. You can read the code, but here are some key points to look for. You'll need to implement them in your own app with your own values and strings (like the names of your columns, table, and database).

Using the Static Values

If you're new this environment, you may have to do a bit of searching to find the many static variables that are used. Here's a quick guide to where they may be.

Static Values May Be in the APIs

The android.provider.BaseColumns API is used by Android content providers throughout the system. Structured data is used throughout Android and many other operating systems (the Cocoa and Cocoa Touch table classes provide somewhat similar functionality). In the example code, two static values from BaseColumns are used frequently. Both are strings. _COUNT is the number of rows in a directory, and _ID is a unique id for a row.

Static Values May Be in Imported Files.

NotePad.java contains the NotePad class. That class itself contains the NoteColumns class. It contains these static values (among others):

```
public static final String TITLE = "title";
public static final String NOTE = "note";
public static final String CREATED_DATE = "created";
public static final String MODIFIED_DATE = "modified";
```

Static Values May Be in the Main File

Here are some static values from the NoteBookProvider class in NoteBookProvider.java.

```
private static final String TAG = "NotePadProvider";
private static final String DATABASE_NAME = "notepad.db";
private static final int DATABASE_VERSION = 2;
private static final String NOTES_TABLE_NAME = "notes";
private static HashMap<String, String> sNotesProjectionMap;
```

```
private static HashMap<String, String> sLiveFolderProjectionMap;
private static final int NOTES = 1;
private static final int NOTE_ID = 2;
private static final int LIVE_FOLDER_NOTES = 3;
private static final UriMatcher sUriMatcher;
```

Extend SQliteOpenHelper

You'll need to declare a class that extends SQLiteOpenHelper and implement your own onCreate function. Following is the code you need to work with in the example:

```
private static class DatabaseHelper extends SQLiteOpenHelper {
  DatabaseHelper(Context context) {
    super(context, DATABASE_NAME, null, DATABASE_VERSION);
  }

  @Override
  public void onCreate(SQLiteDatabase db) {
    db.execSQL("CREATE TABLE " + NOTES_TABLE_NAME + " ("
      + NoteColumns._ID + " INTEGER PRIMARY KEY,"
      + NoteColumns.TITLE + " TEXT,"
      + NoteColumns.NOTE + " TEXT,"
      + NoteColumns.CREATED_DATE + " INTEGER,"
      + NoteColumns.MODIFIED_DATE + " INTEGER"
      + ");");
  }
  // The code above will create this where COLid is the value of
  // NoteColumns._ID at runtime
  // CREATE TABLE notes (COLid INTEGERPRIMARYKEY, title TEXT,
  //   note TEXT, created INTEGER, modified INTEGER);

  @Override
  public void onUpgrade(SQLiteDatabase db, int oldVersion, int newVersion) {
    Log.w(TAG, "Upgrading database from version " + oldVersion + " to "
      + newVersion + ", which will destroy all old data");
    db.execSQL("DROP TABLE IF EXISTS notes");
    onCreate(db);
  }
}
private DatabaseHelper mOpenHelper;
```

The line shown in bold is easily missed. It's used throughout the example code in this file: It's the local version of SQLiteOpenHelper. With this structure, if you reuse this code, you can make changes within DatabaseHelper (e.g., your own string names) while doing very little to the rest of the code.

Next is code from the example that uses the boilerplate code you'll reuse. Note the use of mOpenHelper which is DatabaseHelper. As you can see, it builds on what has already been constructed. If you examine the full code in the example, you'll see that most of the code deals with the data to be stored rather than the SQLite interface.

The code in bold is the code that actually updates the database. The db.insert method constructs the necessary SQLite syntax using the static values described previously in this chapter. The code directly below the bold code takes the return value from db.insert and puts it into a local variable called rowId. That's exactly what it is—the unique id of the new row. If the process fails, -1 is returned.

```java
@Override
public Uri insert(Uri uri, ContentValues initialValues) {
  // Validate the requested uri
  if (sUriMatcher.match(uri) != NOTES) {
    throw new IllegalArgumentException("Unknown URI " + uri);
  }
  ContentValues values;
  if (initialValues != null) {
    values = new ContentValues(initialValues);
  } else {
    values = new ContentValues();
  }

  Long now = Long.valueOf(System.currentTimeMillis());
  // Make sure that the fields are all set
  if (values.containsKey(NoteColumns.CREATED_DATE) == false) {
    values.put(NoteColumns.CREATED_DATE, now);
  }
  if (values.containsKey(NoteColumns.MODIFIED_DATE) == false) {
    values.put(NoteColumns.MODIFIED_DATE, now);
  }
  if (values.containsKey(NoteColumns.TITLE) == false) {
    Resources r = Resources.getSystem();
    values.put(NoteColumns.TITLE, r.getString(android.R.string.untitled));
  }
  if (values.containsKey(NoteColumns.NOTE) == false) {
    values.put(NoteColumns.NOTE, "");
  }

  SQLiteDatabase db = mOpenHelper.getWritableDatabase();
  long rowId = db.insert(NOTES_TABLE_NAME, NoteColumns.NOTE, values);
  if (rowId > 0) {
    Uri noteUri = ContentUris.withAppendedId(NoteColumns.CONTENT_URI, rowId);
    getContext().getContentResolver().notifyChange(noteUri, null);
    return noteUri;
  }
  throw new SQLException("Failed to insert row into " + uri);
}
```

Summary

This chapter shows you the basics of working with the SQLite built-in database in Android. Although there's a lot of code in the example shown here, only a few lines of code are actually what you need to write for the SQLite interface. When you reuse the code for your own purposes, most of the code you write will be related to your own app and its data rather than to the database.

■ ■ ■

CHAPTER 8

Using SQLite with Core Data (iOS and OS X)

Although SQLite is integrated tightly with PHP, Android, and iOS/OS X, the integration strategies differ somewhat. In a way, they form a logical progression. PHP supports SQLite as an extension to the language (no longer optional as of this writing). When you write your PHP code for SQLite, today's best practice is to use the PHP data object (PDO) class. However, the rest of your code may very well be traditional procedural code: there is no assumption that you will be writing object-oriented code throughout.

Android represents a slightly different approach to the idea of creating a general-purpose class (android.database). In the case of Android, a specific subclass database provides SQLite support (android.database.sqlite) along with the generalized data management support in android.database.

It's reasonable to think of SQLite in Android as a more object-oriented implementation than that of PHP. (This is a generalization and is not meant to ignore—or fan—arguments.) Despite these differences in approach, the SQLite code that you've seen in this book and other places is visible both in PHP and in Android in many cases. You'll find familiar SQLite commands in the source code for PHP and Android apps—commands such as SELECT, DELETE, INSERT INTO, DELETE FROM, and so forth.

Over in the world of iOS and OS X, the object-oriented approach goes deeper. Under normal circumstances, you as a developer don't even see SQLite code. As is the case with PDO and android.database, there are common classes that are customized for various databases, but the SQLite code is placed inside these common classes and is rarely visible to you. This means that you're not writing statements or commands such as SELECT, DELETE, and so forth. Instead, you're writing code that interacts with the common classes and their subclasses for your app.

Furthermore, there is one really critical distinction between the implementation in PDO and android.database when compared to iOS and OS X. That difference has to do with relationships which are conceptually exactly the same as they are in any other SQL environment, but they are implemented in a very different way which you'll see in this chapter.

Finally, there's a key point that is critical to Core Data but doesn't apply in the same way to the other environments. PDO and android.database wrap specific databases and provide access to them. Core Data works with a variety of databases, but its database accesses go through Core Data itself: the underlying database is not exposed. Some people think of Core Data itself as a database, but it is not. Technically, it is an object graph and persistence framework. It uses a database (or, in the case of SQLite, a database library), but it is not a database itself. Its job is to hide the database so you can work with the objects that Core Data manages based on data in the database it uses.

■ **Note**   Core Data can work with a variety of databases including SQLite, but in wrapping those databases in its own framework classes, it provides some consistency across different database types. Thus, although in the most common uses of Core Data on iOS and OS X it is SQLite that is the underlying database, you can't simply slide an existing SQLite database into Core Data. If you have an existing database (SQLite or any other) and want to move it to Core Data, the simplest way is to unload it and reload it into the Core Data model that you create. You can do this using utilities for the unload in many cases; the reloading may require a brief section of code to interact with Core Data. Having the facilities to unload and reload databases of any type is a best practice in all cases. It can come in handy not only for moving from one database manager to another but also for debugging, auditing, and other needs.

This chapter focuses on the common framework that uses SQLite for OS X and iOS and shows you how to work with it.

Introducing the Core Data Framework

The common code that is (very) roughly analogous to PDO and android.database is the Core Data framework. It consists of a number of classes—this chapter describes the key classes along with the graphical editor for a data model.

WHERE CORE DATA CAME FROM

Core data is a *framework*—a collection of classes that work together and can be installed together in your app. It is used with Cocoa (the user interface (UI) framework for OS X) and Cocoa Touch (the UI framework for iPad, iPod touch, and iPhone). It's also used with tvOS and watchOS. It provides a fully object-oriented interface to standard databases. It was originally written at NeXT in 1994 as Enterprise Objects Framework (EOF), and it supported Oracle, Sybase, Informix, and ODBC-compliant servers along with OpenBase Lite. Today, it supports the built-in SQLite library on all the platforms as well as XML on Mac.

Core Data descends from EOF, but it is very different in many ways. Among the major similarities that remain are the graphical user interface for describing relational data. Today, it is part of Xcode as Data Model Inspector and Xcode Core Data model editor.

- Both are totally object-oriented with the stored objects and their properties being represented graphically in the Xcode Core Data model editor although you can write code to manage them if you want. If you do write code, it is standard Objective-C or Swift code rather than SQL or SQLite.

- In addition to the stored objects and properties themselves, the graphical user interface used to design the data, its objects, and their relationships descends directly from EOF tools. You can write code to manage the data and its objects, but that code is Swift or Objective-C and not SQL or SQLite.

Perhaps the most important aspects of both EOF and Core Data are very much related.

There are three aspects of Core Data that matter to you as a developer.

- The graphical user interface for building and maintaining a data model including relationships. This is the *Xcode Core Data model editor*. It runs inside Xcode.

- The runtime objects that make Core Data work for you. They are collectively referred to as the *Core Data stack*.

- Other objects that you frequently use with Core Data.

This chapter addresses the first one. Chapter 9 discusses the second and third.

Using the Core Data Model Editor

Start with an Xcode project either from a built-in Xcode template or from your own project. Many of the built-in templates have an option to use Core Data when you set up the project. If you have chosen this option, you have a data model already in your project. Otherwise, you need to add a data model to your project. Use File->New->File to open the sheet shown in Figure 8-1 and select Data Model from the Core Data section for iOS, watchOS, tvOS, or OS X as appropriate.

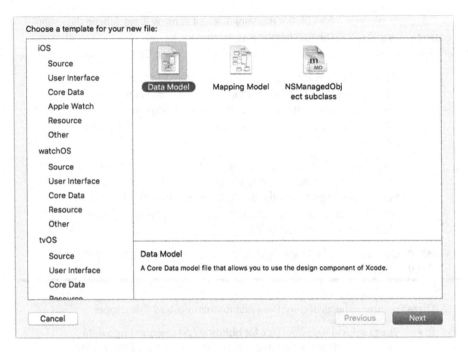

Figure 8-1. *Add a new data model to your project*

■ **Note**   Data Model editor is built into Xcode, the integrated development environment for Apple projects. This chapter assumes you know the basics of Xcode. If you don't, visit developer.apple.com to find the documentation and download Xcode. It's also available for free in the Mac App Store.

You start from an empty data model as shown in Figure 8-2.

Figure 8-2. *Start from a new data model*

The center of the Core Data model editor lets you create your data model. There are two styles you can use for the editor: a *table style* and a *graph style* (you'll see both later in this section). When you are working on a data model, there's a Data Model inspector available at the right of the editing window. It will contain relevant data for anything that you have selected in the Core Data model editor. (In the case of Figure 8-2, nothing is selected that has additional information.)

At the left of the Data Model editor, you have three sets of objects you can manage.

- **Entities** are SQLite tables behind the scenes.

- **Fetch requests** are prepared queries similar to those you can create in SQLite. They can contain variables that are substituted at query time.

- **Configurations** are used internally. For basic development, you don't need to do anything because the default configuration will work.

To add a new object to the Core Data model editor, you can use the + button at the lower left of the window. The small down-pointing triangle next to the + lets you choose to add an entity, fetch request, or configuration. Your choice is sticky—this means that after you've chosen to add a fetch request, the + will add other fetch requests until you change the default.

Using Entities

After you add a new entity, it will appear in the center of the editing window with its three sections (see Figure 8-3):

- **Attributes** are SQLite columns behind the scenes.

- **Relationships** are the logical relationships you're used to in SQL. In Core Data, they have a fundamental difference which is explained in "Managing Relationships" later in this chapter.

- **Fetched properties** allow you to fetch properties from a different persistent store. They are for advanced users and aren't covered in this introduction to Core Data.

Figure 8-3. *Add a new entity*

Perhaps the most important aspect of an entity is that, when you fetch it at runtime, it is fetched as an instance of NSManagedObject (or a subclass thereof). As a result of that fetch, the entity becomes a class instance, and its attributes become properties of the instance. You'll see how to create subclasses in Chapter 9.

■ **Note**   Actually, when you fetch an object with Core Data, it is initially fetched as a *fault*. That's not an error. It represents the absolutely bare minimum of information that Core Data needs to proceed. Basically, it is an instance of `NSManagedObject` or a subclass thereof but without the persistent properties filled in. This means that you can use it in some ways, but when you actually need the data, the fault is said to *fire*, and the data is filled in. When the fault has fired and the data has been filled in, the fault is said to be *realized*. This happens behind the scenes, so you don't need to be aware of it except that in looking at debugging statements, get used to recognizing that in the context of Core Data, "fault" doesn't mean an error. Faulting is one of the ways in which Core Data optimizes performance.

When you select an entity in the sidebar, you see its details in the center of the editing window. You can add new attributes using the + below the attributes table. Initially, each attribute will have a placeholder name such as `attribute` or `attribute1`. To add details to your entity (or to any other object selected in the Core Data model editor), select it and open the Data Model inspector at the right of the window as shown in Figure 8-4.

Figure 8-4. *Use the Data Model inspector*

You can rename the entity. You can also provide additional details that are useful in using it with your code. There are more details on this topic in Chapters 9 and 10.

Working with Attributes

You can (and should) rename your attributes using meaningful names. (See sidebar "Naming Core Data Model Objects.")

NAMING CORE DATA MODEL OBJECTS

By convention, Core Data entity names begin with a capital letter. Furthermore, they are typically singular. Thus, an entity that keeps track of users would typically be called User and an entity that keeps track of scores for users would typically be called Score.

If you have a to-many relationship from User to Score so that one user can have many scores, the *relationship* is named scores (plural).

These have been conventions for some time in Core Data (and they're not unlike conventions and best practices in other environments. With Xcode Core Data, this convention has become a requirement: you can't name an entity user (lowercase), and you can't name an attribute in that entity to Name (uppercase).

Note that although the Core Data conventions are similar to conventions in other environments, that similarity extends to the existence of standards for capitalization, number (plural/singular), and so forth. The details such as whether or not to capitalize do vary.

Each attribute must have a type. The types that are available in Core Data are as follows:

- Integer16, Integer32, and Integer64
- Decimal
- Double
- Float
- String
- Boolean
- Binary Data
- Transformable

There is an initial Undefined value, but when you try to save the data model, you'll be required to change it to an appropriate value.

■ **Tip** These types apply to Core Data no matter what data management tool you use to manage its persistent stores. If you compare this list to the list of types in SQLite, you can see that because these types don't provide a one-to-one match to SQLite types, Core Data itself must provide the mapping. In practice, this means that type checking is done in Core Data, and it is stricter than SQLite libraries alone where one of the guiding principles is that "any column can still store any type of data" (www.sqlite.org/datatype3).

The Transformable data type is just what its name implies: you can transform one type to another. It's typically used to store data types such as images and other resources that can be stored as a generic data type and then used by the app directly as the resource type with Core Data providing the transformation in both directions behind the scenes.

Figure 8-5 shows attributes and their types for an entity. Note that when first created, it is called `Entity`. You can rename it by double-clicking it in the sidebar.

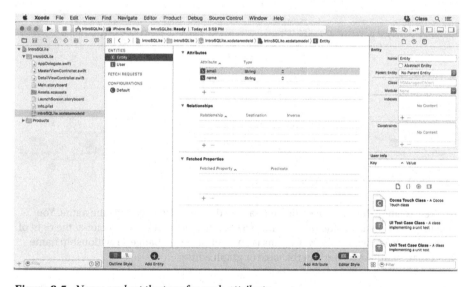

Figure 8-5. *Name and set the type for each attribute*

Managing Relationships

When you design a relational database, you set up relationships among your data objects. There are many ways of drawing these relationships on paper, on white boards, or in various graphical relational data editors. These relationships are implemented in queries when you write a clause such as

```
WHERE department.employee_name = corporate.manager_name
```

In Core Data, relationships are part of the data model. Core Data manages them (it generates the WHERE clauses as needed). This means you don't have to write the WHERE clauses yourself (in part because you don't write SQLite syntax yourself so there's no place to write them). Once you have two entities created in your data model, you can build a relationship between them using the Xcode Core Data model editor. (Yes, you can create self-joins within a single table, but that's a more advanced topic.)

The easiest way to create a relationship is to switch to the graph style (using the Editor Style controls at the lower right of the editing area). You may have to rearrange the entities so that it's easy to see the two you care about at the same time. Then, control-drag from one entity to the other as shown in Figure 8-6.

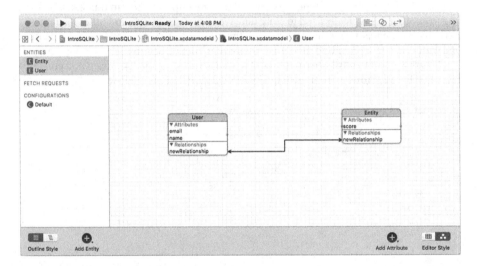

Figure 8-6. *Create a relationship*

New relationships are given default names: double-click to change the name. You need to specify details of the relationship, so open the Data Model inspector at the right of the window as shown in Figure 8-7. This is another place to change a relationship name rather than double-clicking it in the table or graph editor.

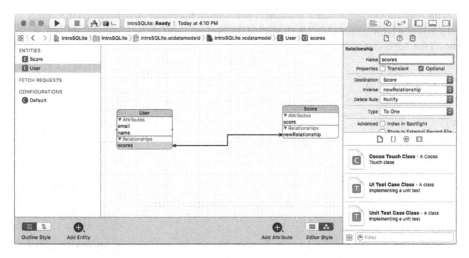

***Figure 8-7.** Refine your relationships*

Relationships are bidirectional, but you configure each side of the relationship in the graph view and then modify it in the Data Model inspector. Figure 8-7 shows the `scores` relationship highlighted. The most important item in the Data Model inspect is the name. You can change it here or by double-clicking it in the graph view.

You frequently want to change the Type setting, switching between `To One` and `To Many`. As you do, you'll see the arrows at the end of the relationship change from single to double arrows (this is standard relational diagram notation).Type is sometimes referred to as *cardinality.*

Figure 8-8 shows a new relationship from `User` to `Score` that is a `to-many` relationship (note the double arrows); the inverse is a `to-one` relationship (note the single arrow on the `User` side).

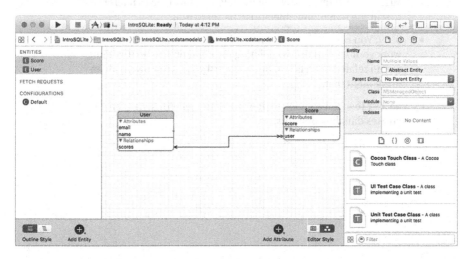

***Figure 8-8.** Specify the cardinality of relationships*

71

In configuring relationships, people often switch back and forth between the graph view and the table view using the control at the bottom right of the window. Figure 8-9 shows the table view.

Figure 8-9. Use the table view for relationships

Delete rules let you specify what happens when you try to delete one end of the relationship. In brief, you can specify that deleting the source of a relationship can have any of these outcomes:

- Cascade. Deleting one end of the relationship deletes all related objects.

- Nullify. Deleting one end of the relationship, causes references to it in the remaining object(s) to be set to null.

- Deny. You can't delete one end of the relationship. You have to work your way up to it by deleting the child objects so that there are no related objects left, but you must write your own code to implement that.

- No Action. You can delete one end of the relationship even if it creates dangling pointers.

Summary

This chapter provides an introduction to Core Data, the framework that implements access to SQLite for OS X, iOS, watchOS, and tvOS. You've seen how to build your data model using Xcode Data Model editor, and how to build relationships that are implemented for you when Core Data creates the appropriate WHERE clauses in the SELECT statements it produces and runs.

Compared to PHP and Android, this aspect of SQLite data modeling is much more graphical than text oriented. However, if you like writing traditional code, have no fear. Chapters 9 and 10 show the Objective-C and Swift code to implement your SQLite data model.

CHAPTER 9

■ ■ ■

Using SQLite/Core Data with Swift (iOS and OS X)

After looking at the Xcode Core Data model editor which lets you build your Core Data environment graphically, it's time to move to the code that implements it. Core Data wraps the persistent store, which in many cases is the built-in SQLite library for OS X, iOS, watchOS, and tvOS.

This chapter looks at the Core Data stack—the objects that do the work in all cases. It also looks at the specific objects that you may use in implementing your own app.

The SQLite syntax that is exposed in other environments is still working here, and, as you saw in Chapter 8, in the discussion of data types, SQLite is doing the work.

Looking at the Core Data Stack

The Core Data stack is a set of three objects that work together to provide functionality. They are as follows:

- **Managed Object Model**. This is what you saw built graphically in Chapter 8. It's very similar to what is often referred to as a database schema. (A schema is described in a formal language rather than graphically.) Remember that relationships are explicitly defined in a Core Data data model whereas in SQLite (and in SQL in general) the relationships are implemented in the WHERE clauses that you write.

- **Persistent Store Coordinator**. Each SQLite table is usually represented as a persistent store in Core Data. This one-to-one correspondence of persistent store and database table is sufficient in most cases. However, you can have multiple persistent stores to improve performance or provide other optimizations. As far as the Core Data stack is concerned, one of the three key elements is a persistent store coordinator which coordinates all of the persistent stores for a given Core Data app.

In most cases, the persistent store coordinator handles a single persistent store. However, the full name (persistent store coordinator) is still used because in more complex solutions the persistent store coordinator does actually manage several persistent stores. It is the persistent store coordinator and its persistent stores that do the transformation from the flat SQLite database file to the objects that you work with in your Core Data app. Accordingly, there are options you use when you create a persistent store that specify what the underlying data is (XML on OS X, SQLite on any of the platforms, in-memory stores, and others that may be created in the future).

The defined store types are

- `NSSQLiteStoreType`

- `NSXMLStoreType` (OS X)

- `NSBinaryStoreType` (OS X)

- `NSInMemoryStoreType` (OS X)

- **Managed Object Context.** A managed object context is like a scratch pad: it contains data that has been retrieved from a persistent store and that has (perhaps) been modified by your app. When you are finished with modifications, you save the managed object context. If you want to cancel the operation, you simply destroy the managed object context.

The Core Data stack consists of these three objects, and they relate to one another to create a single entity.

Fetching Data to the Core Data Stack

Fetch requests can be created in Xcode Core Data model editor or in your code. They retrieve data from a persistent store (through a persistent store coordinator) and place it in a managed object context. Fetch requests are not part of the Core Data stack, and that fact is reflected in the standard architecture for Core Data (described in the following section).

Structuring a Core Data App

The basic Core Data stack (persistent store coordinator, data model, and managed object context) typically is placed in a location that is available throughout the app. The most common case (used in Master-Detail Application and Single View Application templates built into Xcode) places the Core Data stack in `AppDelegate`. `AppDelegate` typically creates views and other objects within the app. If they will need parts of the Core Data stack, `AppDelegate` passes them down to the views either when they are created or when `AppDelegate` is managing them after they have been created by others.

Passing a Managed Object Context to a View Controller in iOS

Here is how the Master-Detail Application template for iOS passes the managed object context to the view. (As is the case with Apple's code samples and much new code that's written today, this is Swift code.)

```
func application(application: UIApplication,
  didFinishLaunchingWithOptions
    launchOptions: [NSObject: AnyObject]?) -> Bool {

  // Override point for customization after application launch.
  let splitViewController = self.window!.rootViewController
    as! UISplitViewController
  let navigationController =
    splitViewController.viewControllers[splitViewController.
    viewControllers.count-1]
    as! UINavigationController
  navigationController.topViewController!.navigationItem.leftBarButtonItem =
    splitViewController.displayModeButtonItem()
  splitViewController.delegate = self

  let masterNavigationController = splitViewController.viewControllers[0]
    as! UINavigationController
  let controller = masterNavigationController.topViewController
    as! MasterViewController
  controller.managedObjectContext = self.managedObjectContext
  return true
}
```

The views are created from a storyboard, and this code starts from the basic window and steps down until it finds the navigation controller at the left of the split view controller. From there, it steps down to the MasterViewController inside the navigation controller. Having gotten that controller, it then sets the managedObjectContext property of MasterViewController to the managedObjectContext created in the Core Data stack in AppDelegate (that is the line of code shown in bold). This is the standard way of doing this.

You can also get to the Core Data stack by finding the app delegate and then accessing one of the stack objects from inside the AppDelegate. This breaks the idea of encapsulation because you're looking inside the app delegate. However, you'll find some sample code that does this in various places, and a (weak) argument can be made for doing it this way if you only rarely—like once—need to access the stack. Here's the code for this other way of getting to the stack.

```
let appDelegate = UIApplication.sharedApplication().delegate as! AppDelegate
// use appDelegate.managedObjectContext or some other stack property
```

Setting Up the Core Data Stack in AppDelegate for iOS

This code is from the Single View Application template that's built into Xcode. It consists of lazy var declarations for the following:

- applicationDocumentsDirectory. This is the directory in which your data model will be placed inside your app. It's just a utility function.

- managedObjectModel

- persistentStoreCoordinator

- managedObjectContext

- By using lazy vars, the initialization code only runs when you actually need it. Thus, this code in the template would never run unless you use Core Data. The comments from the template code are included here.

Creating `applicationDocumentsDirectory` in iOS

This code uses the default file manager to find the document directory for your app. If you want to change the location of your data model's directory, change it here in the code shown in bold. Either use a different directory or create one of your own (and be careful when you're not using the default directory).

```
lazy var applicationDocumentsDirectory: NSURL = {
    // The directory the application uses to store the Core Data store file.
    // This code uses a directory named "com.champlainarts.
       SingleViewCoreDataSwift"
    // in the application's documents Application Support directory.

    let urls = NSFileManager.defaultManager().
       URLsForDirectory(.DocumentDirectory, inDomains: .UserDomainMask)

    return urls[urls.count-1]
}()
```

Creating `managedObjectModel` in iOS

Here the managedObjectModel code is created as needed. The line shown in bold is created when you use the template. If you change your project's name, change this line of code. Also note that, by default, the Core Data model is stored in the app bundle. The xcdatamodeld file that you build with Xcode Core Data model editor is compiled into a momd file during the build process.

```
lazy var managedObjectModel: NSManagedObjectModel = {
    // The managed object model for the application. This property is not
        optional.
    // It is a fatal error for the application not to be able to find
    // and load its model.

    let modelURL = NSBundle.mainBundle().URLForResource
      ("SingleViewCoreDataSwift", withExtension: "momd")!
    return NSManagedObjectModel(contentsOfURL: modelURL)!
}()
```

Creating `persistentStoreCoordinator` in iOS

This code creates a persistent store coordinator based on your managed object model.
The second line shown in bold is created based on your project name, and it contains the
location of the SQLite database file. You normally don't move this file, but this is another
place where you might have to change the file name if you have changed the project name.

Note that in using the data model, if self.managedObjectModel does not exist yet, it
will be created after the reference here.

It's also worth pointing out the line where the SQLiteStoreStype is chosen for the
new persistent store. It's shown in the third bold line.

```
lazy var persistentStoreCoordinator: NSPersistentStoreCoordinator = {
    // The persistent store coordinator for the application. This
        implementation
    //  creates and returns a coordinator, having added the store for the
    // application to it. This property is optional since there are
    // legitimate error conditions that could cause the creation of the
    // store to fail.

    // Create the coordinator and store

    let coordinator = NSPersistentStoreCoordinator
      (managedObjectModel: self.managedObjectModel)

    let url = self.applicationDocumentsDirectory.
      URLByAppendingPathComponent("SingleViewCoreData.sqlite")

    var failureReason = "There was an error creating or loading the
      application's saved data."

    do {
      try coordinator.addPersistentStoreWithType
        (NSSQLiteStoreType, configuration: nil, URL: url, options: nil)
      } catch {
```

```swift
// Report any error we got.

var dict = [String: AnyObject]()

dict[NSLocalizedDescriptionKey] =
  "Failed to initialize the application's saved data"
dict[NSLocalizedFailureReasonErrorKey] = failureReason
dict[NSUnderlyingErrorKey] = error as NSError

let wrappedError = NSError(domain: "YOUR_ERROR_DOMAIN",
                            code: 9999,
                        userInfo: dict)

// Replace this with code to handle the error appropriately.
// abort() causes the application to generate a crash log
// and terminate. You should not use this function in a
// shipping application, although it may be useful during development.

NSLog("Unresolved error \(wrappedError),
  \(wrappedError.userInfo)")

    abort()
  }

  return coordinator
}()
```

If you are not familiar with Swift 2, you may not have seen the do/try/catch block. That is used increasingly in modern Swift code, so this code can serve as a template for other do/try/catch code you may write. The heart of it is in the catch section. The important part of that code is the following:

1. Catch the error.

2. Create an empty dictionary (var dict in this case).

3. Populate the dictionary. This code will be customized for your purposes.

4. Create a new NSError instance with the domain, code, and dictionary that you created in items 2 and 3.

5. Report the error and dictionary using NSLog.

Creating managedObjectContext in iOS

Finally, the managed object context is created. (Note that because of lazy initialization, "finally" may not be accurate because the sequence of creating the Core Data stack components varies depending on which one is the first one accessed.)

```
lazy var managedObjectContext: NSManagedObjectContext = {
  // Returns the managed object context for the application
  // (which is already bound to the persistent store coordinator
  // for the application.) This property is optional since there
  // are legitimate error conditions that could cause the creation
  // of the context to fail.

  let coordinator = self.persistentStoreCoordinator
  var managedObjectContext = NSManagedObjectContext
    (concurrencyType: .MainQueueConcurrencyType)
  managedObjectContext.persistentStoreCoordinator =
    coordinator
  return managedObjectContext
}()
```

Setting Up the Core Data Stack in AppDelegate for OS X

This code is from the Cocoa Application for OS X template that's built into Xcode. It consists of lazy var declarations for the following:

- applicationDocumentsDirectory. This is the directory in which your data model will be placed inside your app.

- managedObjectModel

- persistentStoreCoordinator

- managedObjectContext

By using lazy vars, the initialization code only runs when you actually need it. Thus, this code in the template would never run unless you use Core Data. The comments from the template code are included here.

Creating applicationDocumentsDirectory in OS X

This code differs from iOS to reflect the fact that the file structures differ. Its purpose is the same. The code shown in bold is created from your settings when you set up the project. If you change your developer ID or project name, you may have to change this.

```
lazy var applicationDocumentsDirectory: NSURL = {
  // The directory the application uses to store the Core Data
  // store file. This code uses a directory named
  // "com.champlainarts.OSXProjectSwift" in the user's Application Support
  //   directory.

  let urls = NSFileManager.defaultManager().
    URLsForDirectory(.ApplicationSupportDirectory, inDomains: .UserDomainMask)
```

```
    let appSupportURL = urls[urls.count - 1]

    return appSupportURL.URLByAppendingPathComponent
      ("com.champlainarts.OSXProjectSwift")
}()
```

Creating `managedObjectModel` in OS X

The code is the same as it is for iOS except for the name of the project. The code that is shown in bold for iOS would change for OS X to this (assuming your project name is appropriate).

```
let modelURL = NSBundle.mainBundle().URLForResource
  ("OSXProjectSwift", withExtension: "momd")!
```

Creating `persistentStoreCoordinator` in OS X

```
lazy var persistentStoreCoordinator: NSPersistentStoreCoordinator = {
    // The persistent store coordinator for the application. This
    // implementation creates and returns a coordinator, having added the
    // store for the application to it. (The directory for the store
    // is created, if necessary.) This property is optional since
    // there are legitimate error conditions that could cause the
    // creation of the store to fail.

    let fileManager = NSFileManager.defaultManager()
    var failError: NSError? = nil
    var shouldFail = false
    var failureReason = "There was an error creating or loading
      the application's saved data."

    // Make sure the application files directory is there
    do {
      let properties = try
        self.applicationDocumentsDirectory.resourceValuesForKeys
        ([NSURLIsDirectoryKey])
        if !properties[NSURLIsDirectoryKey]!.boolValue {
          failureReason = "Expected a folder to store application data,
            found a file \(self.applicationDocumentsDirectory.path)."
        shouldFail = true
        }
    } catch {
      let nserror = error as NSError
```

```swift
        if nserror.code == NSFileReadNoSuchFileError {
        do {
                try fileManager.createDirectoryAtPath(self.
                applicationDocumentsDirectory.path!,
                withIntermediateDirectories: true, attributes: nil)
            } catch {
                failError = nserror
            }
        } else {
            failError = nserror
        }
    }

    // Create the coordinator and store
    var coordinator: NSPersistentStoreCoordinator? = nil
    if failError == nil {
        coordinator = NSPersistentStoreCoordinator(managedObjectModel:
        self.managedObjectModel)
        let url = self.applicationDocumentsDirectory.URLByAppending
        PathComponent("CocoaAppCD.storedata")
        do {
            try coordinator!.addPersistentStoreWithType(NSXMLStoreType,
            configuration: nil, URL: url, options: nil)
        } catch {
            failError = error as NSError
        }
    }

    if shouldFail || (failError != nil) {
        // Report any error we got.
        var dict = [String: AnyObject]()
        dict[NSLocalizedDescriptionKey] = "Failed to initialize the
        application's saved data"
        dict[NSLocalizedFailureReasonErrorKey] = failureReason
        if failError != nil {
            dict[NSUnderlyingErrorKey] = failError
        }
        let error = NSError(domain: "YOUR_ERROR_DOMAIN", code: 9999,
        userInfo: dict)
        NSApplication.sharedApplication().presentError(error)
        abort()
    } else {
        return coordinator!
    }
}()
```

Creating `managedObjectContext` in OS X

This code is the same as in iOS.

Creating a Fetch Request in iOS

In iOS, the standard practice is to create the Core Data stack in the app delegate as shown previously in this chapter in "Structuring a Core Data App.: In addition to the Core Data stack, you typically use fetch requests to fetch data from the persistent store into the managed object context. (On OS X, you use binding instead of view controllers and fetch requests.)

This code is fairly common. Here, it is used to fetch all entities with a given name (Event). The entity description is retrieved from the managed object context (the line is shown in bold) and the fetched results controller is created with a reference to that managed object context. A backing variable for the fetchedResultsController is created with the name _fetchedResultsController. This design pattern is frequently use: if the backing variable (starting with the underscore) exists, it is returned on request. If it does not exist, the fetched results controller is created and the underscore backing variable is set to it for the next time it's needed.

```
var fetchedResultsController: NSFetchedResultsController {
  if _fetchedResultsController != nil {
    return _fetchedResultsController!
  }

  let fetchRequest = NSFetchRequest()
  // Edit the entity name as appropriate.
  let entity = NSEntityDescription.entityForName("Event",
    inManagedObjectContext: self.managedObjectContext!)
  fetchRequest.entity = entity

  // Set the batch size to a suitable number.
  fetchRequest.fetchBatchSize = 20

  // Edit the sort key as appropriate.
  let sortDescriptor = NSSortDescriptor(key: "timeStamp", ascending: false)

  fetchRequest.sortDescriptors = [sortDescriptor]

  // Edit the section name key path and cache name if appropriate.
  // nil for section name key path means "no sections".

  let aFetchedResultsController = NSFetchedResultsController(
          fetchRequest: fetchRequest,
     managedObjectContext: self.managedObjectContext!,
        sectionNameKeyPath: nil,
             cacheName: "Master")
```

```
aFetchedResultsController.delegate = self
_fetchedResultsController = aFetchedResultsController

do {
  try _fetchedResultsController!.performFetch()
} catch {
  // Replace this implementation with code to handle the
  // error appropriately.
  // abort() causes the application to generate a crash log
  // and terminate. You should not use this function in a
  // shipping application, although it may be useful during development.

  print("Unresolved error \(error), \(error.userInfo)")
  abort()
}

  return _fetchedResultsController!
}

var _fetchedResultsController: NSFetchedResultsController? = nil
```

If you have created a fetch request in your data model as described in Chapter 8, you can use it to create a fetchedResultsController.

Saving the Managed Object Context

Although this is basically the same in iOS and OS X, there are some minor differences.

Saving in iOS

The last part of Core Data in the app delegate is the utility code to save the context and its changes. If you don't save the managed object context, the changes are gone.

```
func saveContext () {
  if managedObjectContext.hasChanges {

    do {
      try managedObjectContext.save()
    } catch {

      // Replace this implementation with code to handle the error
         appropriately.
      // abort() causes the application to generate a crash log and
         terminate. You
      // should not use this function in a shipping application, although it
      // may be useful during development.
```

```
      let nserror = error as NSError
      NSLog("Unresolved error \(nserror), \(nserror.userInfo)")
      abort()
    }
}
```

This is one of the main reasons for passing the managed object context to views that are created or managed by the app delegate (see the section "Passing a Managed Object Context to a View Controller in iOS"). If the view has the managed object context, as it is processing changes to the view, it can save those changes with managedObjectContext.save.

Here is the standard code from a view controller that can save data.

```
do {
  try context.save()
  } catch {
    // Replace this implementation with code to handle the error
    // appropriately.
    // abort() causes the application to generate a crash log
    // and terminate. You should not use this function in a
    // shipping application, although it may be useful during development.

    print("Unresolved error \(error), \(error.userInfo)")
    abort()
  }
}
```

Saving in OS X

With the menu bar and its commands in OS X, you often are using a Save action to save data. Here is a typical saveAction function from OS X.

```
@IBAction func saveAction(sender: AnyObject!) {
  // Performs the save action for the application, which is to send the
    save: message
  // to the application's managed object context. Any encountered errors are
    presented
  // to the user.

  if !managedObjectContext.commitEditing() {
    NSLog("\(NSStringFromClass(self.dynamicType))
      unable to commit editing before saving")
    }
```

```
if managedObjectContext.hasChanges {
    do {
        try managedObjectContext.save()
    } catch {
        let nserror = error as NSError
        NSApplication.sharedApplication().presentError(nserror)
    }
}
}
```

Working with NSManagedObject

In any app that uses Core Data, you'll need a Core Data stack, and you create it pretty much the same way each time except that you do customize the name of your project. (If you're building your app from one of the built-in Xcode templates, there may be a Core Data check box you can use to automatically insert the Core Data stack code as well as your project name.)

But what about your data? That's going to be managed by your Core Data stack, but surely it requires special coding. The fact is that, as is often the case with Core Data, the SQLite syntax is handled for you behind the scenes. You already have a data model (either from the template as-is or with your modifications) and if you don't, you need to create a data model using File ➤ New ➤ File.

■ **Note** In OS X, view controllers are not generally used; instead, bindings are used. That topic is covered in developer.apple.com.

Each entity in your data model will be transformed into an instance of a class at runtime. Each of those instances is an instance of NSManagedObject or a descendant thereof. This section shows you the basics.

The examples in this section use the same two entities that have been used previously in this book: User and Score. Figure 9-1 shows them in the Xcode Core Data model editor graph view.

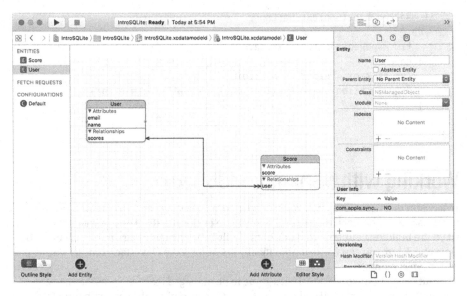

Figure 9-1. *User and Score entities in a data model*

Creating a New NSManagedObject Instance

There are several ways to create new Core Data instances. One of the most common is found in the Master-Detail Application template for iOS. Here's the code that is used there. It is connected to a + in the `MasterViewController` view. Users can tap + to create a new object.

```
func insertNewObject(sender: AnyObject) {
  let context = self.fetchedResultsController.managedObjectContext
  let entity = self.fetchedResultsController.fetchRequest.entity!

  let newManagedObject =
    NSEntityDescription.insertNewObjectForEntityForName(entity.name!,
    inManagedObjectContext: context)

  do {
    try context.save()
  } catch {
    abort()
  }
}
```

You use this code (or code very much like it) whenever you create a new `NSManagedObject`. The beginning of this code just locates the managed object context. It might be a property in the class you're working with such as a `fetchedResultsController`. If it isn't you may need to add a local property which is created (or passed through) when your class is instantiated or when the instance is loaded from a storyboard.

Next, you create an entity description, a subclass of NSEntityDescription. This encapsulates the entity information that you manage in your data model. In the code shown here, the entity description (called entity) is retrieved from a fetched results controller.

The third line of the code actually creates a new instance called newManagedObject. That line of code is worth examining in detail. It's really quite simple, but it's the heart of Core Data.

```
let newManagedObject =
    NSEntityDescription.insertNewObjectForEntityForName(entity.name!,
    inManagedObjectContext: context)
```

You use a class method of NSEntityDescription to create the new object—insert NewObjectForEntityForName. You need the name of the new object to be created and you need the managed object context into which to put it.

If you know the name of the object you want to create, you can omit the line creating entity (the second line of this code) and change this line of code to refer to it by name as in the following snippet.

```
let newManagedObject =
    NSEntityDescription.insertNewObjectForEntityForName("User",
    inManagedObjectContext: context)
```

Obviously, this code is less reusable, but it works.

After you have created that new managed object you save the managed object context into which you inserted it.

```
do {
    try context.save()
  } catch {
    abort()
  }
}
```

As noted in comments through the template code as well as elsewhere in this book, don't use abort() in a shipping app. Instead, catch the error and log it, let the user know that there's a problem (if the user can do something about it), or just fix the problem in your code.

That's all it takes to create a new managed object.

If you want to set a value for an attribute defined for the entity in your data model, you can use key-value coding to do so with a line of code such as the following:

```
newManagedObject.setValue("New User", forKey: "name")
```

If the value to which you set the property is invalid, the save of the managed object context will fail. This will happen particularly if you've declared validation rules in the Xcode Data Model editor. Until you shake down the validation rules, you may have to deal with errors appropriately. (And, of course, if you are allowing user input, a whole host of user-generated errors may occur.)

■ **Tip**   If you really want to gain an appreciation of Core Data, work through the SQLite syntax that must be generated behind the scenes to implement the code shown here. It definitely is being executed, but you don't have to type it in.

Working with a Subclass of NSManagedObject

You can create a subclass of NSManagedObject instead of using an instance of NSManagedObject itself. If you create a subclass (the process is described next), the chief benefit is that instead of using key-value coding, you can set a value for newManagedObject using code such as the following:

```
newManagedObject.name = "New User"
```

Creating a new subclass of NSManagedObject is easy with Xcode Core Data model editor. Here are the steps involved. Begin with your data model open as shown in Figure 9-1. (It doesn't matter if you're looking at the graph or table view.) Choose Editor ➤ Create NSManagedObject Subclass to open the window shown in Figure 9-2. Select the data model you want to use as shown in Figure 9-2. (Typically there's only one. There may be several if you have been modifying your data model.)

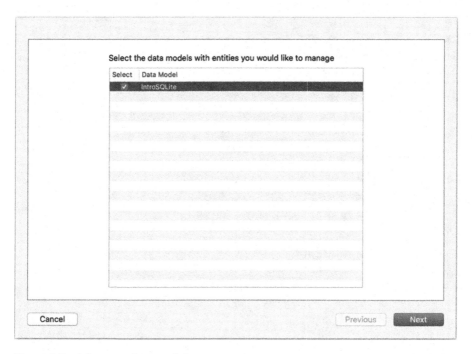

Figure 9-2. Select your data model

After you click Next, choose the entity or entities you want to subclass (see Figure 9-3). By default, the entity or entities that you have selected in the graph or table view (as shown in Figure 9-1) are selected here. You don't have to subclass everything. Sometimes, you choose to subclass the more complex entities and leave the others as NSManagedObject instances.

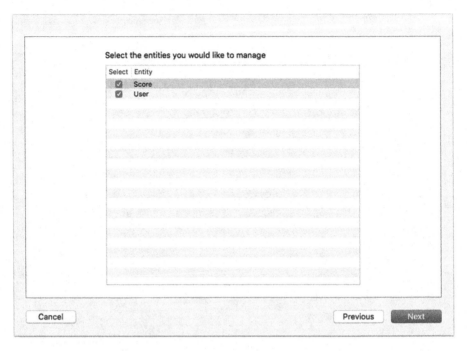

Figure 9-3. *Choose the entities to subclass*

Click Next and choose where to save your new files as shown in Figure 9-4. Also choose the language you want for the subclass files. (You can mix and match Swift and Objective-C.)

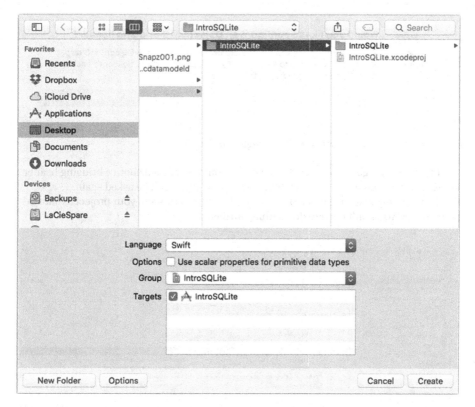

Figure 9-4. *Choose where to save the subclass files and what language you want to use*

You should double-check the group (for the Navigator) and the target, but usually they're correct. The option for scalar properties requires a little explanation. By default, your entity attributes are converted into Swift or Objective-C properties using the native Cocoa or Cocoa Touch types. Thus, a Double is converted to NSNumber. NSNumber is a much more powerful construct than Double (for one thing, it's a class). If you're working a lot with such a property, sometimes the power of NSNumber gets in the way. Choosing to use scalar types will use the basic platform (non-object) types (such as Double) which may make your code simpler.

If your project is basically written in Swift and you choose to create your subclass in Objective-C, you may be asked if you want to create a bridging header between the two languages as shown in Figure 9-5. Yes, you do want to do this.

Figure 9-5. *You can choose to create a bridging header*

In a mixed-language project, don't worry if you're not asked about a bridging header. It only need to be created once, so after the first time, you won't be asked again.

The bridging header is created for you in the Build Settings of your project as shown in Figure 9-6. You don't need to do anything further.

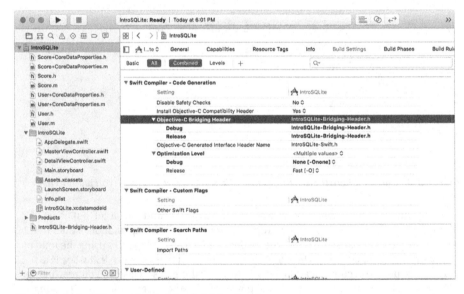

Figure 9-6. *Building settings with a bridging header*

If you're creating a Swift subclass, Xcode will create two files for each entity you have selected. The first is the basic file for the class (User in this case): it's empty, and looks as follows:

```
import Foundation
import CoreData

class User: NSManagedObject {

// Insert code here to add functionality to your managed object subclass

}
```

It will be named `User.swift`. As the comment in the code indicates, you can add any code that you want to this new class that you've created.

The companion file that Xcode creates for you is a *class extension*. (A Swift class extension is like an Objective-C category but without a name.) Its name will be in the following form:

```
User+CoreDataProperties.swift
```

The contents of the file will be as follows:

```
import Foundation
import CoreData

extension User {

    @NSManaged var name: String?
    @NSManaged var email: String?
    @NSManaged var scores: NSManagedObject?
}
```

At runtime, the extension is merged with the basic class, so you're able to access the name property for an instance of `User` by writing

```
myName.name = "test"
```

That's all it takes to create an `NSManagedObject` subclass.

■ **Note**   To see how to use your subclasses, see Chapter 12.

Summary

This chapter shows you how to work with SQLite/Core Data on OS X and iOS using Swift—the more modern of languages for Cocoa and Cocoa Touch. There is still plenty of Objective-C code around, and Chapter 10 shows that code.

CHAPTER 10

■ ■ ■

Using SQLite/Core Data with Objective-C (iOS and Mac)

The Core Data stack described in detail in Chapter 9 is front and center in this chapter but in the context of Objective-C. Yes, using Swift and Objective-C with SQLite are very similar processes, but the details of the implementation are just different enough that they're treated in separate chapters so that you can find what you're looking for without flipping back and forth. If you've already read Chapter 9 (or, conversely, if you've read Chapter 10 before you get to Chapter 9), feel free to skip anything that's redundant as you become bilingual in SQLite and both Apple languages.

Objective-C is the original language for what has become Cocoa and Cocoa Touch. It was designed for NeXTSTEP in the early 1980s. This was the time when object-oriented programming was becoming the primary way of developing software. A variety of languages were designed to implement this new paradigm. Some were built from the ground up, and others were built on top of then-existing languages such as C. (There even is an Object COBOL language.)

Objective-C was the only language for development on NeXTSTEP and later Cocoa and Cocoa Touch. In 2014, Swift was added to the mix. Like Objective-C before it, it is based on the programming styles and languages of the time, but in the case of Swift, those languages are "Objective-C, Rust, Haskell, Ruby, Python, C#, CLU, and far too many others to list," according to Chris Lattner as quoted in Wikipedia. (Lattner was the original developer of Swift.)

There are important differences in the languages' implementations of the Core Data stack, but the architecture is the same for both.

Looking at the Core Data Stack

The Core Data stack is a set of three objects that provide functionality. They are as follows:

- **Managed Object Model**. This is what you saw built graphically in Chapter 8. It's very similar to what is often referred to as a database schema. (A schema is described in a formal language rather than graphically.) Remember that relationships are explicitly defined in a Core Data model whereas in SQLite (and in SQL in general) the relationships are implemented in the WHERE clauses that you write.

- **Persistent Store Coordinator**. Each SQLite table is usually represented as a persistent store in Core Data. This one-to-one correspondence of persistent store and database table is sufficient in most cases. However, you can have multiple persistent stores to improve performance or provide other optimizations. As far as the Core Data stack is concerned, one of the three key elements is a persistent store coordinator which coordinates all of the persistent stores for a given Core Data app.

  In most cases, the persistent store coordinator handles a single persistent store. However, the full name (persistent store coordinator) is still used because in more complex solutions the persistent store coordinator does actually manage several persistent stores. It is the persistent store coordinator and its persistent stores that do the transformation from the flat SQLite database file to the objects that you work with in your Core Data app. Accordingly, there are options you use when you create a persistent store that specify what the underlying data is (XML on OS X, SQLite on any of the platforms, in-memory stores, and others that may be created in the future).

  The defined store types are

  - `NSSQLLiteStoreType`

  - `NSXMLStoreType` (OS X)

  - `NSBinaryStoreType` (OS X)

  - `NSInMemoryStoreType` (OS X)

- **Managed Object Context**. A managed object context is like scratch pad: it contains data that has been retrieved from a persistent store and that has (perhaps) been modified by your app. When you are finished with modifications, you save the managed object context. If you want to cancel the operation, you simply destroy the managed object context.

The Core Data stack consists of these three objects, and they relate to one another to create a single entity.

Fetching Data to the Core Data Stack

Fetch requests can be created in Xcode Core Data model editor or in your code. They retrieve data from a persistent store (through a persistent store coordinator) and place it in a managed object context. Fetch requests are not part of the Core Data stack, and that fact is reflected in the standard architecture for Core Data (described in the following section).

Objective-C Highlights

Swift looks in many ways like other programming languages you are probably familiar with, but there are some differences. Objective-C looks particularly different to many people. Here are some of the major differences. There is more information on developer.apple.com about Objective-C. Also, the code snippets in this chapter will give you some key examples, but the focus here is on SQLite and its syntax as well as on Core Data.

Using Quoted Strings

In Objective-C, a quoted string is introduced with @ as in @"myString".

Objective-C Is a Messaging Language

The most important difference is that Objective-C is a *message-based* language, and it is *dynamic*. In many object-oriented programming languages today, you call methods or functions of a class with syntax such as

```
myObject.myFunction ();
```

Instead of calling a *function* or *method* (the terms are used interchangeably here although there are some very subtle differences), with Objective-C, you send a *message* to an object. The message might actually have a name that makes you think it's a function call, but deep down it isn't. In Objective-C, the previous line of code would be written as

```
[myObject myFunction];
```

The myFunction *message* is sent to myObject.

Using Brackets in Objective-C

As you can see in the previous section, Objective-C looks different. Message are enclosed in brackets. The recipient is the first item within the brackets, and the message selector is the second. (A message selector identifies the message to be sent. It often looks like the name of a function or method but it is not a quoted string.) Either the recipient or the message selector can be an expression which is evaluated at runtime—hence it is dynamic.

Brackets have long been an issue for some people when they look at Objective-C. For that reason, there have been a couple of variants. After Apple purchased NeXT, *modern syntax* was introduced alongside the classical Objective-C brackets. That particular variant is no longer supported, but Objective-C 2.0 (2006) introduced *dot syntax* in which the brackets are replaced by a more accessible syntax. Both of these variants can function alongside classical Objective-C notation because they do not change what happens inside the compiler. The code in the section "Passing a Managed Object Context to a View Controller in iOS" uses dot syntax for Objective-C.

Chaining Messages

As is the case in Swift and other languages, you can chain statements together if they produce a result. Thus, you can write this code (assuming that myFunction returns an object that can respond to myFunction2).

```
((myObject.myFunction ()).myFunction2 ()
```

That is the same as writing

```
x = myObject.myFunction ();
y = x.myFunction2 ();
```

And, in Objective-C you can write

```
[[myObject myFunction] myFunction2]
```

This is the same as writing

```
x = [myObject myFunction];
y = [x myFunction2];
```

Ending Statements with a Semicolon

Objective-C statements end with a semicolon. (You can end a Swift statement with a semicolon, but it's optional. It is required if you have two Swift statements on one line: the first statement is separated from the second with a semicolon.)

Separating Headers and Bodies in Objective-C

In Swift and many other modern languages, there is a single file for each class. In Objective-C there are two files—a header file with a .h extension and a body file with a .m extension.

Looking at Method Declarations

The syntax for method declarations is different from Swift. The quickest way to see the difference is to look at the examples in the section "Setting Up the Core Data Stack in AppDelegate for iOS."

Handling `nil` in Objective-C

In object-oriented languages, there are often references to instances of objects which, in most cases, are stored on the *heap* (i.e., in an area of memory that can be used as needed by the app). It is different from the *stack* which is a last in-first out (LIFO) abstract memory structure. ("Abstract" in the sense that it behaves as if it was a single structure but it need not be in some implementations.) Stack data typically belongs to a specific function so that when the function completes, the stack can be *cut back* with its variables removed from memory.

Instances of objects are allocated in the heap and are not automatically cut back. They need to be removed by one means or another. In Objective-C, several strategies to clean up unused memory have been implemented over time. The current version relies on reference counting: when an instance is allocated, its reference count is set to 1. Every time that instance is used, the using code typically increases the reference count. When each code use of the instance completes, the reference count is reduced by 1. When the reference count reaches 0, the operating system can reuse the memory.

This memory management strategy relies on software engineers to manage the reference counts. Over time, automated and semi-automated tools have been provided. However, you can still find code with the primary memory management tools: `retain` and `release` which increase and decrease the reference count by 1.

With automatic reference counting (ARC), a great deal of this is automated.

In Objective-C, instances of objects are accessed with pointers. The traditional C language pointer syntax (an asterisk—*) is used. Thus, you will see declarations in Objective-C such as

```
NSView *myView;
```

or

```
NSView* myView;
```

The location of the asterisk doesn't matter. This declares a pointer variable called `myView` which points to an instance of `NSView`.

Probably.

Rather than pointing to an instance of `NSView`, `myView` could be `nil`. You'll find plenty of code in Objective-C to test if a pointer is nil before using it. That's a good practice.

In the lifetime of an Objective-C object, it can pass through several states. First, it is declared as in

```
NSView *myView;
```

Then it is initialized to something. This can happen in a separate statement or in a combined statement.

```
NSView *myView;
myView = nil;
```

or

```
NSView *myView = nil;
```

If there is a period of time between the declaration and its being set to something valid (such as nil or an actual instance), the pointer is undefined. If you use it, your app's behavior could be anything, but "crash" is likely to be part of the description. The problem of dangling pointers in Objective-C has existed for many years, and there have been many ways to address it. Today, with Objective-C, ARC is the primary way in which the problem is addressed. With Swift, this is one of the primary reasons for implementing optionals—so that it's impossible to have these dangling pointers.

If you're coming from another language, the square brackets and the use of nil (and the necessity of initializing pointers properly) may be the two biggest changes you have to get used to when referring to Core Data objects which may or may not exist (the nature of databases, like that of networks, means that you can't rely on things being in existence).

Structuring a Core Data App with Objective-C

The basic Core Data stack (persistent store coordinator, data model, and managed object context) typically is placed in a location that is available throughout the app. The most common case (used in Master-Detail Application and Single View Application templates built into Xcode) places the Core Data stack in AppDelegate. AppDelegate typically creates views and other objects within the app. If they will need parts of the Core Data stack, AppDelegate passes them down to the view controllers and views either when they are created or when AppDelegate is managing them after they have been created by others.

Passing a Managed Object Context to a View Controller in iOS

Here is how the Master-Detail Application template for iOS passes the managed object context to the view controller. (This code uses Objective-C dot syntax.)

```
(BOOL)application:(UIApplication *)application
  didFinishLaunchingWithOptions:(NSDictionary *)launchOptions {

  // Override point for customization after application launch.
  UISplitViewController *splitViewController =
    (UISplitViewController *)self.window.rootViewController;
  UINavigationController *navigationController =
    [splitViewController.viewControllers lastObject];
```

```
navigationController.topViewController.navigationItem.leftBarButtonItem =
    splitViewController.displayModeButtonItem;
splitViewController.delegate = self;

UINavigationController *masterNavigationController =
    splitViewController.viewControllers[0];
MasterViewController *controller = (MasterViewController *)
    masterNavigationController.topViewController;
controller.managedObjectContext = self.managedObjectContext;
return YES;
}
```

The views are created from a storyboard, and this code starts from the basic window and steps down until it finds the navigation controller at the left of the split view controller. From there, it steps down to the MasterViewController inside the navigation controller. Having gotten that controller, it then sets the managedObjectContext property of the masterViewController to the managedObjectContext created in the Core Data stack in AppDelegate. This is the standard way of doing this.

You can also get to the Core Data stack by finding the app delegate and then accessing one of the stack objects. This breaks idea of encapsulation because you're looking inside the app delegate. However, you'll find some sample code that does this in various places, and a (weak) argument can be made for doing it this way if you only rarely—like once—need to access the stack. Here's the code for this other way of getting to the stack.

```
AppDelegate *appDelegate = (AppDelegate *)
    [[UIApplication sharedApplication] delegate];

// use appDelegate.managedObjectContext or some other stack property
```

Setting up the Core Data Stack in AppDelegate for iOS

This code is from the Single View Application template that's built into Xcode. It consists of lazy var declarations for:

- applicationDocumentsDirectory. This is the directory in which your data model will be placed inside your app.

- managedObjectModel

- persistentStoreCoordinator

- managedObjectContext

By using lazy vars, the initialization code only runs when you actually need it. Thus, this code in the template would never run unless you use Core Data.

The comments from the template code are included here.

Creating the App Delegate Header

This is the code to create AppDelegate in Objective-C. Notice that the import statement is different from Swift. Also, the compiler directives such as @property, @interface, and @end are not in Swift. The method declarations (saveContext and applicationDocumentsDirectory) are good examples of declarations in Objective-C.

```
#import <UIKit/UIKit.h>
#import <CoreData/CoreData.h>

@interface AppDelegate : UIResponder <UIApplicationDelegate>

@property (strong, nonatomic) UIWindow *window;

@property (readonly, strong, nonatomic) NSManagedObjectContext
*managedObjectContext;
@property (readonly, strong, nonatomic) NSManagedObjectModel
*managedObjectModel;
@property (readonly, strong, nonatomic) NSPersistentStoreCoordinator
*persistentStoreCoordinator;

- (void)saveContext;
- (NSURL *)applicationDocumentsDirectory;

@end
```

Synthesizing Properties in AppDelegate.m

Properties are declared in header files, but they must be synthesized in the body files. The @synthesize compiler directive typically involves creating a backing variable with the name of the property and accessing it directly when you're in the body. Properties that are exposed in the header file are accessed as properties using dot notation, and behind-the-scenes property accessors work with the backing variables (the underscored variables). Except for special cases such as Core Data, a lot of this is done for you automatically if you want the default backing variable names.

```
@synthesize managedObjectContext = _managedObjectContext;
@synthesize managedObjectModel = _managedObjectModel;
@synthesize persistentStoreCoordinator = _persistentStoreCoordinator;
```

Creating `applicationDocumentsDirectory` in iOS

This code uses the default file manager to find the document directory for your app. If you want to change the location of your data model's directory, change it here in the code shown in bold. Either use a different directory or create one of your own (and be careful when you're not using the default directory).

```
- (NSURL *)applicationDocumentsDirectory {
    // The directory the application uses to store the Core Data store file.
    // This code uses a directory named "com.champlainarts.SingleViewAppOC" in the
    // application's documents directory.

    return [[[NSFileManager defaultManager] URLsForDirectory:NSDocumentDirectory
        inDomains:NSUserDomainMask] lastObject];
}
```

Creating `managedObjectModel` in iOS and OS X

Here the managedObjectModel code is created as needed. The line shown in bold is created when you use the template. If you change your project's name, change this line of code. Also note that, by default, the core data model is stored in the app bundle. The xcdatamodeld file that you build with Xcode Core Data model editor is compiled into a momd file during the build process.

```
- (NSManagedObjectModel *)managedObjectModel {
    // The managed object model for the application. It is a fatal error for the
    // application not to be able to find and load its model.

    if (_managedObjectModel != nil) {
        return _managedObjectModel;
    }

    NSURL *modelURL = [[NSBundle mainBundle] URLForResource:@"SingleViewAppOC"
        withExtension:@"momd"];
    _managedObjectModel = [[NSManagedObjectModel alloc] initWithContentsOfURL
        :modelURL];
    return _managedObjectModel;
}
```

Creating `persistentStoreCoordinator` in iOS

This code creates a persistent store coordinator based on your managed object model. The first line shown in bold is created based on your project name, and it contains the location of the SQLite database file. You normally don't move this file, but this is another place where you might have to change the file name if you have changed the project name.

Note that in using the data model, if self.managedObjectModel does not exist yet, it will be created after the reference here. Notice that this is done differently than it is in Swift.

It's also worth pointing out the line where the SQLiteStoreType is chosen for the new persistent store. It's shown in the second bold line.

```objc
- (NSPersistentStoreCoordinator *)persistentStoreCoordinator {
    // The persistent store coordinator for the application. This
    implementation creates
    // and returns a coordinator, having added the store for the application to it.

    if (_persistentStoreCoordinator != nil) {
        return _persistentStoreCoordinator;
    }

    // Create the coordinator and store

    _persistentStoreCoordinator = [[NSPersistentStoreCoordinator alloc]
        initWithManagedObjectModel:[self managedObjectModel]];
    NSURL *storeURL = [[self applicationDocumentsDirectory]
        URLByAppendingPathComponent:@"SingleViewAppOC.sqlite"];
    NSError *error = nil;
    NSString *failureReason = @"There was an error creating or
        loading the application's saved data.";
    if (![_persistentStoreCoordinator addPersistentStoreWithType:NSSQLiteStoreType
        configuration:nil URL:storeURL options:nil error:&error]) {
        // Report any error we got.
        NSMutableDictionary *dict = [NSMutableDictionary dictionary];
        dict[NSLocalizedDescriptionKey] = @"Failed to initialize the
            application's saved data";
        dict[NSLocalizedFailureReasonErrorKey] = failureReason;
        dict[NSUnderlyingErrorKey] = error;
        error = [NSError errorWithDomain:@"YOUR_ERROR_DOMAIN" code:9999
        userInfo:dict];

        // Replace this with code to handle the error appropriately.
        // abort() causes the application to generate a crash log and terminate. You
        // should not use this function in a shipping application, although it may be
        // useful during development.

        NSLog(@"Unresolved error %@, %@", error, [error userInfo]);
        abort();
    }

    return _persistentStoreCoordinator;
}
```

Creating managedObjectContext in iOS

Finally, the managed object context is created. It incorporates the persistent store coordinator which, in turn, has a reference to the managed object model. Thus, you have the entire Core Data stack.

```
- (NSManagedObjectContext *)managedObjectContext {
  // Returns the managed object context for the application (which is already
  // bound to the persistent store coordinator for the application.)

  if (_managedObjectContext != nil) {
    return _managedObjectContext;
  }

  NSPersistentStoreCoordinator *coordinator = [self persistentStoreCoordinator];
  if (!coordinator) {
    return nil;
  }

  _managedObjectContext = [[NSManagedObjectContext alloc]
    initWithConcurrencyType:NSMainQueueConcurrencyType];
  [_managedObjectContext setPersistentStoreCoordinator:coordinator];

  return _managedObjectContext;
}
```

Setting Up the Core Data Stack in AppDelegate for OS X

This code is from the Cocoa Application for OS X template that's built into Xcode. It consists of declarations that provide similar functionality to lazy var declarations in Swift. The declarations are for the following:

- applicationDocumentsDirectory. This is the directory in which your data model will be placed inside your app.

- managedObjectModel

- persistentStoreCoordinator

- managedObjectContext

Creating applicationDocumentsDirectory in OS X

This code differs from iOS to reflect the fact that the file structures differ. Its purpose is the same. The code shown in bold is created from your settings when you set up the project. If you change your developer ID or project name, you may have to change this.

```
- (NSURL *)applicationDocumentsDirectory {
  // The directory the application uses to store the Core Data store file.
  // This code uses a directory named "com.champlainarts.OSXProjectOC" in
  // the user's Application Support directory.
```

```
NSURL *appSupportURL = [[[NSFileManager defaultManager]
  URLsForDirectory:NSApplicationSupportDirectory inDomains:NSUserDomainMask]
  lastObject];

return [appSupportURL
  URLByAppendingPathComponent:@"com.champlainarts.OSXProjectOC"];
}
```

Creating `managedObjectModel` in OS X

The code is the same as it is for iOS except for the name of the project. The code that is shown in bold for iOS would change for OS X to this (assuming your project name is appropriate).

```
NSURL *modelURL = [[NSBundle mainBundle] URLForResource:@"SingleViewAppOC"
  withExtension:@"momd"];
```

Creating `persistentStoreCoordinator` in OS X

Xcode creates this for you (or you can create it yourself if you're building your own Core Data stack). Note the line in bold: it's taken from your project setup, and you need to change it for your own project.

```
- (NSPersistentStoreCoordinator *)persistentStoreCoordinator {
  // The persistent store coordinator for the application. This implementation
  // creates and returns a coordinator, having added the store for the application
  // to it. (The directory for the store is created, if necessary.)

  if (_persistentStoreCoordinator) {
    return _persistentStoreCoordinator;
  }

  NSFileManager *fileManager = [NSFileManager defaultManager];
  NSURL *applicationDocumentsDirectory = [self applicationDocumentsDirectory];
  BOOL shouldFail = NO;
  NSError *error = nil;
  NSString *failureReason = @"There was an error creating or loading
    the application's saved data.";

  // Make sure the application files directory is there
  NSDictionary *properties = [applicationDocumentsDirectory
    resourceValuesForKeys:@[NSURLIsDirectoryKey] error:&error];
  if (properties) {
```

```
    if (![properties[NSURLIsDirectoryKey] boolValue]) {
      failureReason = [NSString stringWithFormat:
      @"Expected a folder to store application data, found a file (%@).",
      [applicationDocumentsDirectory path]];
      shouldFail = YES;
    }
  } else if ([error code] == NSFileReadNoSuchFileError) {
    error = nil;
    [fileManager createDirectoryAtPath:[applicationDocumentsDirectory path]
      withIntermediateDirectories:YES attributes:nil error:&error];
  }

  if (!shouldFail && !error) {
    NSPersistentStoreCoordinator *coordinator = [[NSPersistentStoreCoordinator alloc]
      initWithManagedObjectModel:[self managedObjectModel]];
    NSURL *url = [applicationDocumentsDirectory
      URLByAppendingPathComponent:@"OSXCoreDataObjC.storedata"];
    if (![coordinator addPersistentStoreWithType:NSXMLStoreType configuration:nil
      URL:url options:nil error:&error]) {
      coordinator = nil;
    }
    _persistentStoreCoordinator = coordinator;
  }

  if (shouldFail || error) {
    // Report any error we got.
    NSMutableDictionary *dict = [NSMutableDictionary dictionary];
    dict[NSLocalizedDescriptionKey] = @"Failed to initialize the application's
      saved data";
    dict[NSLocalizedFailureReasonErrorKey] = failureReason;
    if (error) {
      dict[NSUnderlyingErrorKey] = error;
    }
    error = [NSError errorWithDomain:@"YOUR_ERROR_DOMAIN" code:9999 userInfo:dict];
    [[NSApplication sharedApplication] presentError:error];
  }

  return _persistentStoreCoordinator;
}
```

Creating managedObjectContext in OS X

This code is the same as in iOS.

Creating a Fetch Request in iOS

In iOS, the standard practice is to create the Core Data stack in the app delegate as shown previously in this chapter in " Setting up the Core Data Stack in AppDelegate for iOS" and "Setting Up the Core Data Stack in AppDelegate for OS X." In addition to the Core Data stack, you typically use fetch requests to fetch data from the persistent store into the managed object context. (On OS X, you use binding instead of view controllers and fetch requests.)

This code is fairly common. Here, it is used to fetch all entities with a given name (Event). The entity description is retrieved from the managed object context (the line is shown in bold) and the fetched results controller is created with a reference to that managed object context. A backing variable for the fetchedResultsController is created with the name _fetchedResultsController. This design pattern is frequently use: if the backing variable (starting with the underscore) exists, it is returned on request. If it does not exist, the fetched results controller is created and the underscore backing variable is set to it for the next time it's needed.

```
- (NSFetchedResultsController *)fetchedResultsController
{
  if (_fetchedResultsController != nil) {
    return _fetchedResultsController;
  }

  NSFetchRequest *fetchRequest = [[NSFetchRequest alloc] init];
  // Edit the entity name as appropriate.
  NSEntityDescription *entity = [NSEntityDescription entityForName:@"Event"
    inManagedObjectContext:self.managedObjectContext];
  [fetchRequest setEntity:entity];

  // Set the batch size to a suitable number.
  [fetchRequest setFetchBatchSize:20];

  // Edit the sort key as appropriate.
  NSSortDescriptor *sortDescriptor = [[NSSortDescriptor alloc]
    initWithKey:@"timeStamp" ascending:NO];

  [fetchRequest setSortDescriptors:@[sortDescriptor]];

  // Edit the section name key path and cache name if appropriate.
  // nil for section name key path means "no sections".
  NSFetchedResultsController *aFetchedResultsController =
    [[NSFetchedResultsController alloc]
    initWithFetchRequest:fetchRequest
      managedObjectContext:self.managedObjectContext
```

```
        sectionNameKeyPath:nil cacheName:@"Master"];
    aFetchedResultsController.delegate = self;
    self.fetchedResultsController = aFetchedResultsController;
  NSError *error = nil;
  if (![self.fetchedResultsController performFetch:&error]) {
      // Replace this implementation with code to handle the error appropriately.
      // abort() causes the application to generate a crash log and terminate. You
      // should not use this function in a shipping application, although it may be
      // useful during development.
      NSLog(@"Unresolved error %@, %@", error, [error userInfo]);
      abort();
  }

  return _fetchedResultsController;
}
```

If you have created a fetch request in your data model as described in Chapter 8, you can use it to create a fetchedResultsController.

Saving the Managed Object Context

Although this is basically the same in iOS and OS X, there are some minor differences.

Saving in iOS

```
- (void)saveContext {
  NSManagedObjectContext *managedObjectContext = self.managedObjectContext;
  if (managedObjectContext != nil) {
    NSError *error = nil;
    if ([managedObjectContext hasChanges] && ![managedObjectContext
    save:&error]) {
      // Replace this implementation with code to handle the error appropriately.
      // abort() causes the application to generate a crash log and
      terminate. You
      // should not use this function in a shipping application, although it may be
      // useful during development.
      NSLog(@"Unresolved error %@, %@", error, [error userInfo]);
      abort();
    }
  }
}
```

Saving in OS X

With the menu bar and its commands in OS X, you often are using a Save action to save data. Here is a typical saveAction function from OS X.

```
- (IBAction)saveAction:(id)sender {
  // Performs the save action for the application, which is to send the
  save: message
  // to the application's managed object context. Any encountered errors are presented
  // to the user.

  if (![[self managedObjectContext] commitEditing]) {
    NSLog(@"%@:%@ unable to commit editing before saving", [self class],
      NSStringFromSelector(_cmd));
  }

  NSError *error = nil;
  if ([[self managedObjectContext] hasChanges] && ![[self managedObjectContext]
    save:&error]) {
    [[NSApplication sharedApplication] presentError:error];
  }
}
```

Working with NSManagedObject

In any app that uses Core Data, you'll need a Core Data stack, and you create it pretty much the same way each time except that you do customize the name of your project. (If you're building your app from one of the built-in Xcode templates, there may be a Core Data check box you can use to automatically insert the Core Data stack code as well as your project name.)

But what about your data? That's going to be managed by your Core Data stack, but surely it requires special coding. The fact is that, as is often the case with Core Data, the SQLite syntax is handled for you behind the scenes. You already have a data model (either from the template as-is or with your modifications) and if you don't you need to create one using File ➤ New ➤ File.

▪ **Note**   In OS X, view controllers are not generally used; instead, bindings are used. That topic is covered in developer.apple.com.

Each entity in your data model will be transformed into an instance of a class at runtime. Each of those instances is an instance of NSManagedObject or a descendant thereof. This section shows you the basics.

The examples in this section use the same two entities that have been used previously in this book: User and Score. Figure 10-1 shows them in the Xcode Core Data model editor graph view

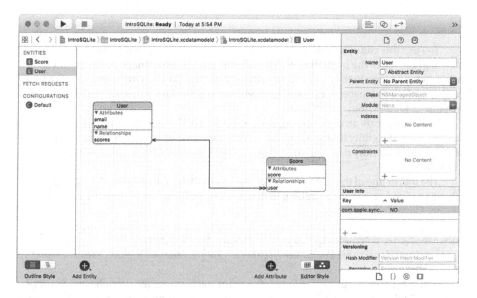

Figure 10-1. *User and Score entities in a data model*

Creating a New NSManagedObject Instance

There are several ways to create new Core Data instances. One of the most common is found in the Master-Detail Application template for Objective-C. Here's the code that is used there. It is connected to a + in the MasterViewController view, but any object in your interface can be connected to an action such as the following. (This happens in MasterViewController.ViewDidLoad).

```
- (void)insertNewObject:(id)sender {
  NSManagedObjectContext *context = [self.fetchedResultsController
    managedObjectContext];
  NSEntityDescription *entity = [[self.fetchedResultsController
  fetchRequest] entity];
```

```
NSManagedObject *newManagedObject = [NSEntityDescription
    insertNewObjectForEntityForName:[entity name] inManagedObjectContext:context];

NSError *error = nil;
if (![context save:&error]) {
    NSLog(@"Unresolved error %@, %@", error, [error userInfo]);
        abort();
    }
}
```

You use this code (or code very much like it) whenever you create a new
NSManagedObject. The beginning of this code just locates the managed object context. It
might be a property in the class you're working with. If it isn't you may need to add a local
property which is created (or passed through) when your class is instantiated or when the
instance is loaded from a storyboard.

Next, you create an entity description, a subclass of NSEntityDescription. This
encapsulates the entity information that you manage in your data model. In the code
shown here, the entity description (called entity) is retrieved from a fetched results
controller.

The fourth line of the code actually created a new instance called newManagedObject.
That line of code is worth examining in detail. It's really quite simple, but it's the heart
of Core Data.

```
NSManagedObject *newManagedObject = [NSEntityDescriprtion
    insertNewObjectForEntityForName:[entity name] inManagedObjectContext:context];
```

You use a class method of NSEntityDescription to create the new object—insertN
ewObjectForEntityForName. You need the name of the new object to be created and you
need the managed object context into which to put it.

If you know the name of the object you want to create, you can omit the line creating
entity (the second line of this code) and change this line of code to refer to it by name.

```
NSManagedObject *newManagedObject = [NSEntityDescriprtion
      insertNewObjectForEntityForName: "User" inManagedObjectContext:context];
```

Obviously, this code is less reusable, but it works.

After you have created that new managed object you save the managed object
context into which you inserted it:

```
NSError *error = nil;
  if (![context save:&error]) {
    NSLog(@"Unresolved error %@, %@", error, [error userInfo]);
      abort();
  }
```

As noted in comments through the template code as well as elsewhere in this book, don't use abort() in a shipping app. Instead, catch the error and log it, let the user know that there's a problem (if the user can do something about it), or just fix the problem in your code.

That's all it takes to create a new managed object.

If you want to set a value for an attribute defined for the entity in your data model, you can use key-value coding to do so with a line of code such as the following:

```
[newManagedObject setValue:["New User" forKey:@"name"];
```

If the value to which you set the property is invalid, the save of the managed object context will fail. This will happen particularly if you've declared validation rules in the Xcode Data Model editor. Until you shake down the validation rules, you may have to deal with errors appropriately. (And, of course, if you are allowing user input, a whole host of user-generated errors may occur.)

■ **Tip**   If you really want to gain an appreciation of Core Data, work through the SQLite syntax that must be generated behind the scenes to implement the code shown here. It definitely is being executed, but you don't have to type it in.

Working with a Subclass of NSManagedObject

You can create a subclass of NSManagedObject instead of using an instance of NSManagedObject itself. If you create a subclass (the process is described next), the chief benefit is that instead of using key-value coding with setValue:forKey: as shown in the previous section, you can set a value for newManagedObject using code such as the following:

```
newManagedObject.name = "New User"
```

Creating a new subclass of NSManagedObject is easy with Xcode Core Data model editor. Here are the steps involved. Begin with your data model open as shown in Figure 10-1. (It doesn't matter if you're looking at the graph or table view.) Choose Editor ➤ Create NSManagedObject Subclass to open the window shown in Figure 10-2. Select the data model you want to use as shown in Figure 10-2. (Typically there's only one. There may be several if you have been modifying your data model.)

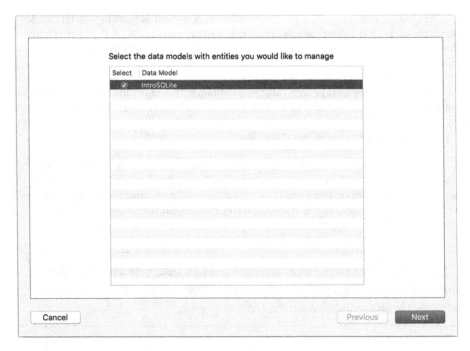

Figure 10-2. *Select your data model*

After you click Next, choose the entity or entities you want to subclass as shown in Figure 10-3. By default, the entity or entities that you have selected in the graph or table view (as shown in Figure 10-1) are selected here. You don't have to subclass everything. Sometimes, you choose to subclass the more complex entities and leave the others as NSManagedObject instances.

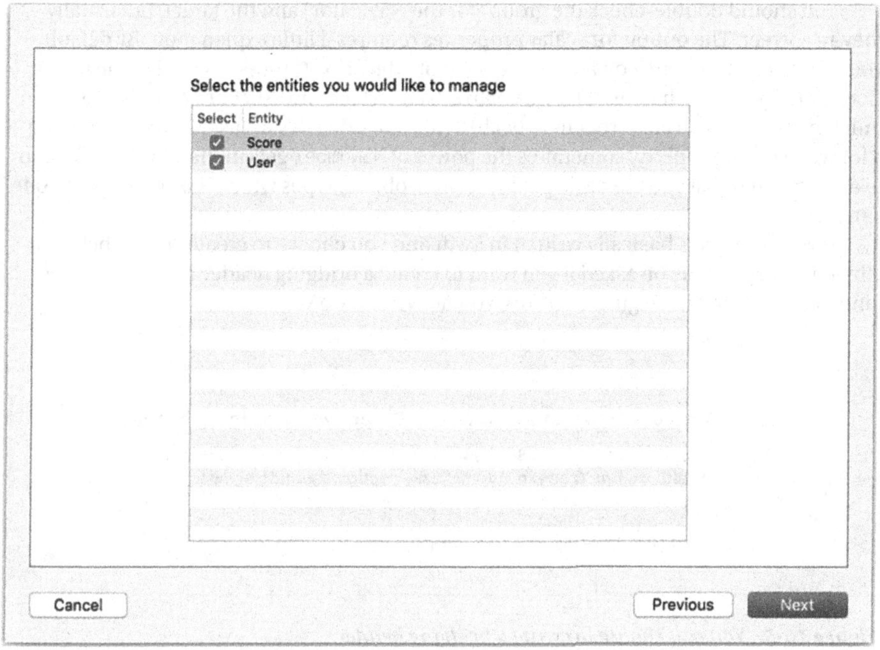

Figure 10-3. *Choose the entities to subclass*

Click Next and choose where to save your new files as shown in Figure 10-4. Also choose the language you want for the subclass files. (You can mix and match Swift and Objective-C.)

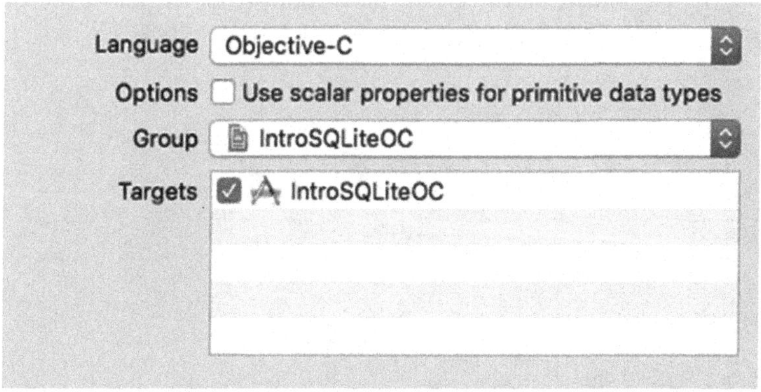

Figure 10-4. *Choose where to save the subclass files and what language you want to use*

You should double-check the group (for the Navigator) and the target, but usually they're correct. The option for scalar properties requires a little explanation. By default, your entity attributes are converted into Swift or Objective-C properties using the native Cocoa or Cocoa Touch types. Thus, a Double is converted to NSNumber. NSNumber is a much more powerful construct than Double (for one thing, it's a class). If you're working a lot with such a property, sometimes the power of NSNumber gets in the way. Choosing to use scalar types will use the basic platform (non-object) types which may make your code simpler.

If your project is basically written in Swift and you choose to create your subclass in Objective-C, you may be asked if you want to create a bridging header between the two languages as shown in Figure 10-5. Yes, you do want to do so.

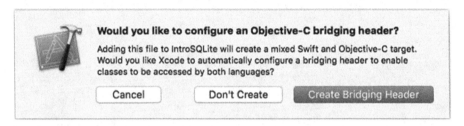

Figure 10-5. *You can choose to create a bridging header*

In a mixed-language project, don't worry if you're not asked about a bridging header. It only need to be created once, so after the first time, you won't be asked.

The bridging header is created for you in the Build Settings of your project as shown in Figure 10-6. You don't need to do anything further.

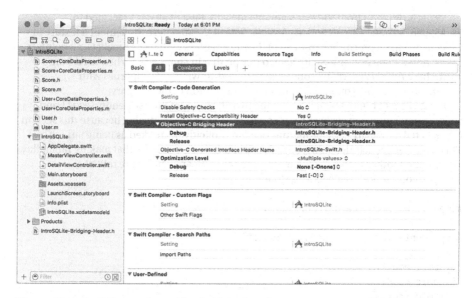

Figure 10-6. *Building settings with a bridging header*

If you're creating an Objective-C subclass, Xcode will create two files for each entity you have selected. As opposed to Swift, these will be the header (.h) and body (.m) files.

The first is the interface file, and it looks as follows:

```
#import "User.h"

NS_ASSUME_NONNULL_BEGIN

@interface User (CoreDataProperties)

@property (nullable, nonatomic, retain) NSString *email;
@property (nullable, nonatomic, retain) NSString *name;
@property (nullable, nonatomic, retain) NSSet<NSManagedObject *> *scores;

@end

@interface User (CoreDataGeneratedAccessors)

- (void)addScoresObject:(NSManagedObject *)value;
- (void)removeScoresObject:(NSManagedObject *)value;
- (void)addScores:(NSSet<NSManagedObject *> *)values;
- (void)removeScores:(NSSet<NSManagedObject *> *)values;

@end

NS_ASSUME_NONNULL_END
}
```

This is different from the extension file in Swift. First of all it is bracketed in NS_ASSUME_NONNULL_BEGIN and NS_ASSUME_NONNULL_END. These implement a feature in Objective-C that comes back from Swift. Inside a section with these brackets, all pointers are assumed to be non-null so it's safe to rely on that in your code. (When used from Swift, these properties will be converted as forced-unwrapped properties with !.)

Inside the .h file you'll see the property declaration of the category (CoreDataProperties) which declares the two attributes of the User entity (email and name). The relationship (scores) comes across as an NSSet. Note that because this section is bracketed as nonnull, the properties need to explicitly be marked as being nullable. This may seem as self-defeating, but as your code grows, you'll see that making nullability an exception rather than a default makes your code cleaner and more robust.

The companion .m file looks as follows:

```
#import "User+CoreDataProperties.h"

@implementation User (CoreDataProperties)

@dynamic email;
@dynamic name;
@dynamic scores;

@end
```

@dynamic represents a promise that the property will be filled in at runtime (when it is retrieved from the persistent store).

That's all it takes to create an NSManagedObject subclass in Objective-C.

■ **Note**   To see how to use your subclasses, see Chapter 12.

Summary

This chapter shows you how to work with SQLite/Core Data on OS X and iOS using Objective-C—the original of language for Cocoa and Cocoa Touch.

■ ■ ■

CHAPTER 11

Using the Simple Database with a PHP Web Site

This book is an introduction to SQLite, but, even though it's just an introduction, the basics of SQLite (and SQL itself which is a key component) aren't particularly complex. True, as you start to build more and more complex apps with more and more features (and more and more robust error checking), your code will get lengthier and more complex. What's attractive to many people about the world of relational databases is that the basic elements are just that—basic. You use and reuse them in various combinations to build more and more powerful apps.

These last two chapters of the *Introducing SQLite* provide you with two apps that are built on SQLite. In this chapter, you'll see how you can build a PHP-based app on SQLite, and in Chapter 12 you'll see how to build a roughly comparable app for iOS.

The app in this chapter has been selected because it demonstrates a number of the features that people want to use as they integrate PHP and SQLite. In particular, you'll see how to retrieve and enter data through the PHP code and SQLite, and you'll see how to handle the integration of SQLite database data with PHP such as in building a drop-down menu (the HTML SELECT element) based on data retrieved from the database.

Reviewing the Database

The data in this chapter is the same relational data that's been used previously in this book, but there are a few tweaks you should be aware of. They are described in this section.

The database consists of three tables that can be used to track values for people. The naming here suggests that they may be used to track scores for users, but that's only one possibility. If you reuse these tables, feel free to rename the properties as you wish. Also, note that by and large *attribute, property, column,* and *field* are used interchangeably to refer to the data stored in a database. *Attribute* is often used in databases, and *property* is used to refer to objects in object-oriented programming. *Column* is used in the context of relational tables, and the use of *field* dates back to paper forms.

■ **Note**   The biggest change in this chapter from previous versions is standardization on capitalization: table names are capitalized, and the names of properties and attributes as well as relationships are not. Where a table contains multiple entries (such as users in the User table), the table name is capitalized and singular. These are styles that are enforced in Apple's Core Data framework, and they are consistent with best practices that many people use. "Many" does not mean all: particularly with regard to whether a table of users is called User or Users, there are two logical approaches to take, and there are many people who argue vehemently for one or the other. Adopting one approach or the other isn't really a solution for many people because we don't work on isolated projects. When client A insists on singular names and client B insists on plural names you often take the most practical approach (use the style that each client wants)

The first table, User, tracks information for people. As set up in this demo, it consists of names and e-mail addresses. It uses a unique rowid for each row. rowid is generated by SQLite. It is shown in Table 11-1.

Table 11-1. *User Table*

rowid	Name	E-mail
1	Rex	rex@champlainarts.com
2	Anni	anni@champlainarts.com
3	Toby	toby@champlainarts.com

The Score table keeps track of values for a user. It references the user in question with the userid attribute. This matches the rowid attribute of the relevant record in User. In that way, you can join the Score and User tables to get both the score and name for an individual (see Table 11-2).

Table 11-2. *Score Table*

userid	score
1	10
2	20
3	30

When the Score and User tables are related based on the userid/rowid relationship, a table like the one shown in Table 11-3 can be created. Note that this is created using WHERE clauses in a SELECT statement: the table only exists at runtime.

Table 11-3. *Related Users and Scores Tables*

Name	Score
Rex	10
Anni	20
Toby	30

If you want to build your table with a tool such as SQLPro for SQLite, the database will look like Figure 11-1 when the Score table is highlighted so you can see its rows (userid and score). rowid (the SQLite-generated primary key) is not shown by default in this display. Also, note that the tables are presented in alphabetical order.

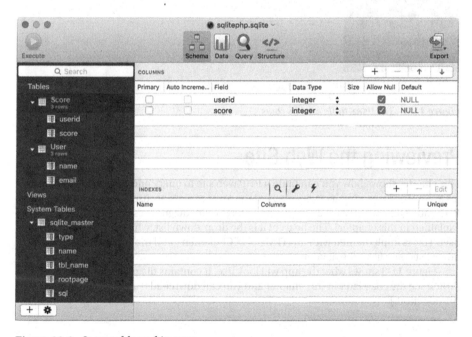

Figure 11-1. *Score table and its rows*

123

In Figure 11-2, you see the User table and its rows.

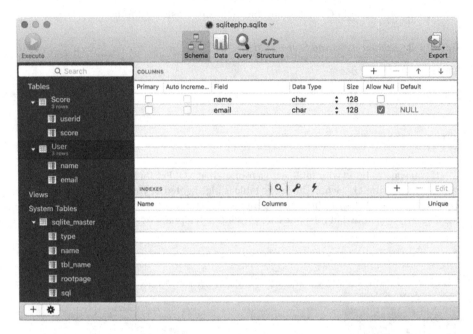

Figure 11-2. The User table and its rows

Previewing the Web Site

This chapter shows how you can build a PHP web site to query and update the database. It's a simple process, but it covers many of the most commonly used aspects of integrating PHP and SQLite. First, you can see a simple page (with diagnostics which will be explained in this chapter). The heart of it is the drop-down list, which lets you select a user. This is implemented with an HTML SELECT element, and the values for the drop-down list come from the database.

Figure 11-3 shows what the app will look like. It contains diagnostic messages. (You'll see the code later in this chapter and you can download it as described in the Introduction.)

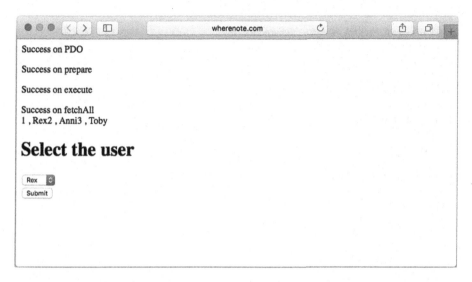

Figure 11-3. *Creating a drop-down list from the database*

In Figure 11-4, you see the data in the table at this point. (Those values of 99 are used for debugging. You'll provide your own data.)

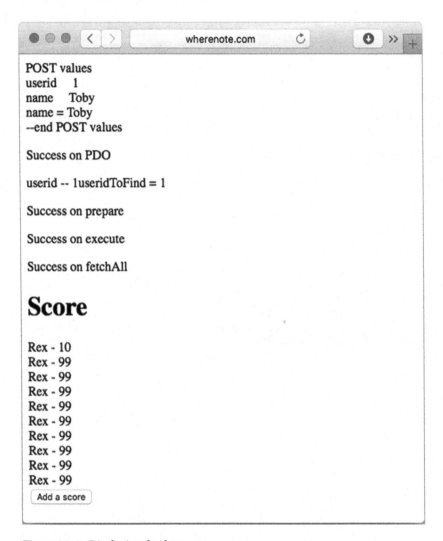

Figure 11-4. Displaying the data

In Figure 11-4 you can see a button to let you add more data. Figure 11-5 shows the result. (Don't worry, the code is shown later in this chapter: there's a lot going on behind the scenes to support that confirmation of adding data.)

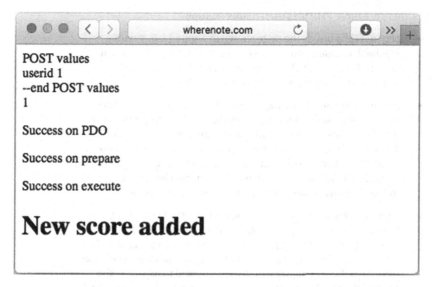

Figure 11-5. You can add new data

Implementing the PHP Web Site

Because the web is designed as a state-less structure, each web page is self-contained. Today, there are many strategies for building continuity into web sites, not the least of which are PHP sessions, cookies, or passing data from one PHP page to another (often with a POST request), but basically each page is still a state-less entity. That means that when you go to a page (i.e., when you run the PHP code that generates the page), the page is generated from data that's in the PHP file and, possibly, retrieved from a database. In the typical pattern, the user clicks a button or uses another interface element to load a new page from PHP code. In order to do this, key data is passed from the first page to the second, or, as noted, relevant data may be cached in cookies or passed in parameters.

■ **Note**   The example used here is called `phpsql`. The various files are numbered 1, 2, and 3. If you are reading on a mobile device, depending on the font you are using, it may not be clear that the file names are a combination of `phpsql` followed by a number. In some fonts, it may look like `phpsq` followed by a two-digit number (the letter L sometimes looks like number 1).

Thus, there are three PHP files used in this example.

- `phpsql1.php` builds the page shown in Figure 11-3. It uses a SQLite database call to retrieve the values for the drop-down menu. When you click Submit, key values (in this case, the selected user) are passed on to the next page.

- `phpsql2.php` builds the page shown in Figure 11-4. It receives the selected user and then queries the database to get the value for the user. As you'll see, this query joins Table 11-1 (User) and Table 11-2 (Score). The name comes from User and the score comes from Score. This join is handled by matching rowid in User to userid in Score (you'll see this later in this chapter). If you click the Add a score button, control passes to the next page.

- `phpsql3.php` adds data for the user selected in Figure 11-3. In order for this to happen, phpql2.php passes the selected userid/rowid to phpsql3.php. Because User and Score have been joined on rowid in User and userid in Score, they have the same value so it doesn't matter which one is passed to phpsql3.php. Each of the files is described in the following sections. You'll find the full code first and then a discussion of the key components.

Looking at the Basic PHP/SQLite Structure

You'll use the same basic structure for all of your PHP/SQLite files. Depending on your preferences, you may use different PHP syntax particularly when it comes to entering HTML that will be passed through (the choice is staying in the world of PHP and using echo or leaving PHP for a section and just using HTML until you need to come back to PHP). Many people use both styles.

Here's the basic structure. (Obviously you'll typically add your own code for the HEAD element and other such parts of the file.) Diagnostics are left in this file. It's easiest to leave them in until you're certain you've got the control flow correct. (Also, remember that the or die syntax is a placeholder for robust error catching with a good user interface.)

```
<html>
 <head>
 </head>

 <body>
 <?php

 $db = 'sqlite:sqlitephp.sqlite';
```

This should be customized to the name of your database. `sqlite:` is part of the PHP data object (PDO) syntax. It must precede the file name.

```
$sqlite = new PDO($db) or die ("<h1>Can't open database</h1>");
echo "<p>Success on PDO</p>";

$query = $sqlite->prepare // insert your query here
```

This should be customized with the query you want to run. At the end of this chapter, you'll see another pattern you can use. Instead of prepare and execute, you can simply execute a single query with the PDO query statement.

```
echo "<p>Success on prepare</p>";
$query->execute() or die ("Can't execute");
echo "<p>Success on execute</p>";

$result = $query->fetchAll() or die ("Can't fetchAll");
echo "Success on fetchAll<br />"; // for debugging
```

Remember that `fetchAll` fetches all the data for the query—not all the data from the table.

```
// Do something with the results. The foreach is just an example.
foreach ($result as $row) {
  echo $row['rowid'], " , ",  $row['name'];
}
```

This section definitely needs to be customized for each use. Here you see a diagnostic that just repeats the data that's been retrieved. It's often useful to use code like this at this point.

```
?>
```

```
<h1>Select the user</h1>
```

```
<form method="post" action="phpsql2.php">
```

Customize this with the name of the next PHP file in the chain (the next page for the user).

```
<?php
  // Here is where you integrate PHP and SQLite - customize as you wish.

  echo '<input type="submit" value="Submit">';
  echo '</form>';
```

If you are using a form, make certain you terminate it and add the Submit button. Note that you can start the form in HTML and finish it in PHP as shown here.

```
?>

</body>
</html>
```

Building the Drop-Down Selection List (`phpsql1.php`)

Here is the full listing of phpsqlite.php. Comments and description are interspersed, but remember to refer to the previous section "Looking at the Basics PHP/SQLite Structure" for general details. This code builds the page shown in Figure 11-3.

```
<html>
 <head>
 </head>
 <body>
 <?php

  $db = 'sqlite:sqlitephp.sqlite';
  $sqlite = new PDO($db) or die ("<h1>Can't open database</h1>");
  echo "<p>Success on PDO</p>";

  $query = $sqlite->prepare ("select name, rowid from User;")
    or die ("<h1>Can't prepare</h1>");
```

The query will be:

```
SELECT name, rowid FROM User;
```

```
  echo "<p>Success on prepare</p>";

  $query->execute() or die ("Can't execute");
  echo "<p>Success on execute</p>";

  $result  = $query->fetchAll() or die ("Can't fetchAll");
  echo "Success on fetchAll<br />";

?>

<h1>Select the user</h1>

<form method="post" action="phpsql2.php">
```

```php
<?php
  echo "<select name='userid'>";
  foreach ($result as $row) {
    echo "<option value = ".$row['rowid'].">".$row['name']."</option>";
  }

   echo '<input type = "hidden" name = "name" value = '.$row["name"].'>';
```

The hidden field is very important: it's the link to the next PHP file (phpsql2.php). The value of name will be retrieved from the POST variables at the beginning of that file. userid is passed in from the SELECT element under the name of userid, and username (used in a title on the next page) is passed in here. The SELECT is visible to the user, but this hidden field is not.

```php
echo '</select> <br >';
echo '<input type="submit" value="Submit">';
echo '</form>';
```

The name of the SELECT element is userid. When the next file unwraps the POST values, it will be the key for the item chosen in the drop-down menu. You may want to customize the Submit button.

```php
?>

</body>
</html>
```

Showing the Selected Data (phpsql2.php)

This is the code to build the page shown in Figure 11-4.

```php
<html>

<head>
</head>

<body>

<?php

  print "POST values<br/>";
  foreach ($_POST as $key => $value) {
    echo "$key     $value <br />";
  }
  print "--end POST values<br/>";

  $name = $_POST['name'];
  print "name = $name <br/>";
```

This code is useful for debugging: it prints out all of the POST keys and values. Remove it when you're happy with the code. Setting the local variable $name is *not* for debugging. The print statement that follows is, but you need to pick up the username from the hidden field on the previous page to show it in a title on this page. You could pick it out of the POST variables when you need it, but many people prefer to unload the POST variables at the beginning of a file.

```php
$db = 'sqlite:sqlitephp.sqlite';
$sqlite = new PDO($db) or die ("<h1>Can't open database</h1>");
echo "<p>Success on PDO</p>";

echo "userid  ".$_POST["userid"];
$useridToFind = $_POST['userid'];
echo "useridToFind = $useridToFind";

$query = $sqlite->prepare ("select name, score from Score s, User u where
s.userid =
  u.rowid and $useridToFind = s.userid ORDER BY Score;") or die
  ("<h1>Can't prepare</h1>");
echo "<p>Success on prepare</p>";

$query->execute() or die ("Can't execute");
echo "<p>Success on execute</p>";

$result  = $query->fetchAll() or die ("Can't fetchAll");
echo "Success on fetchAll<br />"; // for debugging

foreach ($result as $row) {
  echo "<h1>Scores for ".$row['name']." </h1>";
      $userName = $row['name'];
      echo $row['name'], " - ",  $row['score'];
}

echo '<form method="post" action="phpsql3.php">';
echo "<input type='hidden' name='userid' value=$useridToFind>";
```

This is another hidden field — this time passing userid forward to the next PHP file.

```php
  echo '<input type="submit" value="Add a score">';
  echo '</form>';

?>
</body>
</html>
```

Adding New Data (`phpsql3.php`)

Now it's time to add new data to the file. It's a matter of combining basic SQLite syntax for INSERT with the same type of code you've used in previous PHP pages. You should be getting used to this: using PHP and SQLite is the same pattern over and over again.

Following is the code for phpsql3;php:

```
<html>
  <head>
  </head>
  <body>

<?php

print "POST values<br/>";
  foreach ($_POST as $key => $value) {
      echo "$key  $value <br />";
  }
  print "--end POST values<br/>";
  $userid = $_POST["userid"];
  print $userid;
```

This is the same code that provides diagnostics showing all of the POST variables with their keys. Also, note that $userid is set here to be used later in this file. It's the hidden field passed from the previous file copied to a local variable.

```
$db = 'sqlite:sqlitephp.sqlite';
$sqlite = new PDO($db) or die ("<h1>Can't open database</h1>");
echo "<p>Success on PDO</p>";

$query = $sqlite->prepare ("INSERT INTO Score ('score', 'userid') VALUES (99,
  $userid);") or die ("<h1>Can't prepare</h1>");
echo "<p>Success on prepare</p>";
```

This is the heart of the code. Note that 99 is used for debugging. Somewhere in this file you would place your user interface code to provide the actual value. You can do it here, or you can provide the user interface in the previous file (phpsql2.php) in conjunction with the Add a score button. It could bring up a dialog, or it could pick up a value from the current game, or anything that makes sense to you and the user. If you get the value from the previous file, store it in a hidden field and pass it forward as is done with userid and name in other places.

```
$query->execute() or die ("Can't execute");
echo "<p>Success on execute</p>";

//$result  = $query->fetchAll() or die ("Can't fetchAll");
//echo "Success on fetchAll<br />";
```

This code is commented out as a reminder that it's used in cases where you are retrieving data and is *not* needed here. The execute succeeds or fails, but there's no separate result.

```
?>
```

```
<h1>New score added</h1>
```

```
  </body>
  </html>
```

Using Try/Catch Blocks with PHP and PDO

The testing for success used in this file uses traditional PHP and PDO coding. You can use more modern coding with try/catch blocks. (The or die code used as placeholders earlier in this chapter can well be converted to this style.) Following is the general pattern:

```
try {
  $sqlite->query("DELETE FROM Score WHERE rowid = $rowIDToDelete");
} catch (PDOException $e) {
  echo $e->getMessage();
}
```

This code assumes that the Delete button passes the rowid of the score to delete in a hidden field. Remember that rowid is provided by SQLite unless you choose to provide a primary key. Most of the time, you'll find that using the default SQLite rowid is useful for situations like this where you have to delete a given row.

Note, too, that for single queries, this syntax rather than prepare and execute may be simpler to write. When you need to reuse a query, prepare and execute are usually better.

Summary

This chapter provides a simple model for using a SQLite database with PHP. The process is simple.

1. Let the user select data to see.

2. Show the requested data.

3. Allow the user to add new data.

The last step is not required in all cases, but another step often is: allowing the user to delete the requested data that is shown in step 2. You would add a Delete button on that page. Place it inside a form and pass control to another page that does the delete. The delete will look very much like phpsql3.php except that instead of an INSERT, you'll be using DELETE. (There's an example of a DELETE statement in the previous section, "Using Try/Catch Blocks with PHP and PDO.")

■ ■ ■

CHAPTER 12

Using the Simple Database with a Core Data/iOS App

This chapter will show you how to use Core Data to build an iOS app that re-implements the PHP pages shown in Chapter 11. The basics of this app from the Core Data side of things will apply to OS X as well as to iOS, but the Master-Detail Application template is specifically designed to take advantage of the features of iOS. OS X has a separate feature, Bindings, that also very conveniently works together with Core Data. However, it's different from the table-based interface that's used on iOS.

For now it's time to move forward to implement the PHP code in Chapter 11 with Core Data/iOS.

The Story Continues...

Chapter 8 provides a guide to working with the Xcode Core Data model editor. You see the steps involved in creating a new project from the Master-Detail Application template that's part of Xcode and then converting it to a more complex data structure. At the end of the chapter, you have two entities and two relationships connecting them. Figure 12-1 shows the database in the Core Data model editor as it is at the end of Chapter 8. (Note that both Score and User are selected in the sidebar, so the attributes and relationships shown in the editor are those for both of those entities—the union of the attributes and relationships to use database terminology.)

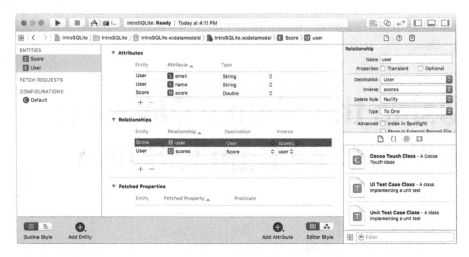

Figure 12-1. *Start from the database from Chapter 9*

If you want to follow along with this chapter, you can either make a copy of that database or download the example file for this chapter. (For this chapter, a new project called Scores has been created but the name of the project is totally up to you.)

The two entities in the Core Data model, User and Score, are the same tables that you've used throughout. One of the important parts of Core Data is that it manages primary and foreign keys for you. SQLite does create a primary key for you (`rowid`) unless you explicitly don't want to use it. Core Data with SQLite does that, too, but it happens behind the scenes. If you open a Core Data SQLite file with a utility, you'll see the keys in the database.

■ **Caution**   You can look at the SQLite databases, but remember that Core Data manages them. Don't make changes to them. In the best of cases, you'll immediately break your Core Data project. In the worst cases, you'll create a time bomb that will go off when you (and your users) least expect it and have the least amount of time to deal with it. If you already have a SQLite database and want to import it to Core Data, the simplest way is to export the data (perhaps to a neutral format like CSV—or comma-separated values) and then to import it into your Core Data app.

Adjusting the Data Model and Template for Core Data

The data model needs to be revised so that it no longer relies on explicit keys (Core Data uses them in the background), and there a few tweaks to the existing code are necessary so that it runs properly.

Getting Rid of Keys and Revising the Data Model

The data model used in Chapter 8 is designed to match basic data that is used in various projects in this book. In this chapter, it's possible to modify that data model to get rid of some excess baggage that Core Data doesn't need. Specifically, the major change you can make is to get rid of the primary keys. Core Data manages its own primary keys, so there's no reason to duplicate that.

"But wait!" you may think. "How do I relate a score to a user without a primary key?"

This question is very common when database-savvy developers first use Core Data. For years (decades, for many) we've relied on those primary keys. Getting rid of them is difficult—it's almost a physical hurt. What's important to remember is that your objective is to relate two entities—in this case a specific score to a specific user. The primary key on one side and the foreign key on the other side make that possible, but they're an implementation issue: what you want to do is relate a specific score to a specific user.

The data model from Chapter 8 (shown here as Figure 12-1) omits those keys—both the primary and foreign keys. The absence of those keys created no difficulty in Chapter 8, and there's no problem now. The table views of the database that have been used until now have been designed to be implemented on various platforms, but for building a Core Data app, they can be revised to omit the no-longer-needed keys.

Changing timeStamp to name

If you've modified the Chapter 9 version of the code or the Xcode Master-Detail Application template, you have probably changed the Event entity to User and replaced the timeStamp date attribute with a name string attribute. It's not necessary to do this in this order, but it's what you may have done. Then, you may have created a new entity, Score.

It's also possible to change Event to Score and create User as a new entity. In another scenario, you can delete Event and create new entities for both User and Score. Either way, you should wind up with the data model shown in Figure 12-1.

Use the find navigator in Xcode to search your project for timeStamp. If you've already changed the data model, the only reference you will find is the initialization code in MasterViewController's insertNewObject function. If you have changed timeStamp to name, you'll wind up with the following line of code:

```
newManagedObject.setValue(NSDate(), forKey: "name")
```

(This code started out with forKey: "timeStamp").

The new attribute is a string, not a date. You can get around this problem quite easily: simply use the description function of most NSObject instances (and their descendants). That function returns a string value of whatever the instance is. Thus, change the line to read

```
newManagedObject.setValue(NSDate().description, forKey: "name")
```

It's still going to set the current date, but this time it will be used as a string (description) rather than a NSDate instance.

Create a New Database on Your Device or Simulator

Remove the app from the simulator or from your device. You'll get a warning that you will remove all its data: that's exactly what you want to do. You've changed the data model, and data that was created with a previous data model won't work. (There are migration routines in Core Data, but they are beyond the scope of *Introducing SQLite*.)

Add the Score Table and Interface to the App

The first step is to see what you have now. Then you can move on to adding Score detail information.

Making Sure You Can Add New Users with + in the Master View Controller

If you're not seeing timestamps when you click + at the top left of the master view controller, you may have replaced the Event entity with Score. The code that controls which entity you create with the + is in fetchedResultController in MasterViewController.swift.

Following is the relevant line of code:

```
let entity = NSEntityDescription.entityForName
  ("User", inManagedObjectContext: self.managedObjectContext!)
```

This started out in the Xcode template as:

```
let entity = NSEntityDescription.entityForName
  ("Event", inManagedObjectContext: self.managedObjectContext!)
```

With your revisions, you may have wound up with:

```
let entity = NSEntityDescription.entityForName
  ("Score", inManagedObjectContext: self.managedObjectContext!)
```

You want to create User entities, so make sure that you revise the code if necessary.

Working with the Detail View

When you run the app now, you'll be able to add new items to the list of users (formerly the list of events but all you've done is change the name). When you add a new user, you can click/tap on it to see its details in the Detail View Controller as shown in Figure 12-2.

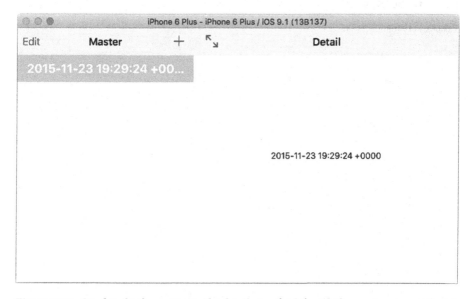

Figure 12-2. *See detail information in the detail view (right) with the master view at the left*

Make certain that what you see matches Figure 12-2 (at least mostly—this is a landscape-oriented iPhone 6 Plus. Once you've done that, you can move on.

Working with the Detail View for Score

The goal here is to replace the existing detail view with a table controller that displays all the scores for a given user and gives you the ability to add new ones. Figure 12-3 shows what you're aiming for.

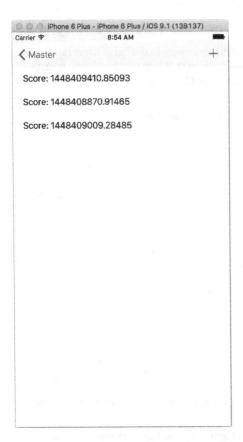

Figure 12-3. *A table-based detail view for scores*

■ **Note** The values for scores are UNIX timestamps (seconds since January 1, 1970). They're easily gotten from NSDate in Cocoa and Cocoa Touch, and they provide different numerical values so you can test your code. The Master View Controller continues to use a timestamp that is displayed as a timestamp.

This will entail three steps:

1. Create subclasses of NSObject for User and Score. (This was described in Chapter 9.)

2. Modify MasterViewController to use the new subclasses.

3. Replace the existing detail view controller in the storyboard with a table-view controller-based detail view controller.

4. Modify the code in DetailViewController to work with the table view controller-based detail view controller.

5. Modify MasterViewController to pass a reference to the current user to the new detail view controller so that its scores can be displayed.

These can be done in any order after Step 1.

Use NSManagedObject Subclasses

The code in MasterViewController creates a new User entity as described in the previous section. Once you have subclasses available, you should use them. In insertNewObject in ManagedObjectController, find the following line of code:

```
let newObject = NSEntityDescription.insertNewObjectForEntityForName
  (entity.name!, inManagedObjectContext: context)
```

Change it to

```
let newUser = NSEntityDescription.insertNewObjectForEntityForName
  (entity.name!, inManagedObjectContext: context) as! User
```

In the line that follows, use the subclass instead of key-value coding. Instead of

```
newManagedObject.setValue(NSDate().description, forKey: "name")
```

Use the new subclass with the following line:

```
newUser.name = NSDate().description
```

Use a Table View Controller for DetailViewController

The easiest way to do this is to remove the current DetailViewController from the storyboard. (It is shown in Figure 12-4.)

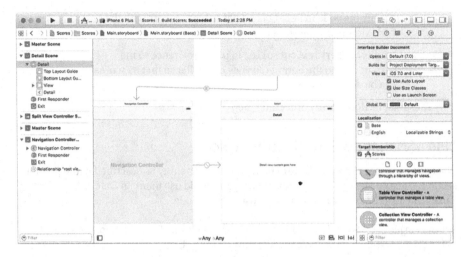

Figure 12-4. *Locate the Detail View Controller in the storyboard and remove it*

Then drag a table view controller from the object library at the right of the window into the storyboard. Place it where the detail view controller was, and control-drag from the navigation controller to the new table view controller. For the relationship, choose *root view controller* (you'll be asked as soon as you release the mouse button on the control-drag).

Modify DetailViewController Code for DetailViewController

There are a few changes to `DetailViewController`.

Using the Subclasses

You need to modify the code so that `DetailViewController` is a subclass of `UITableViewController` rather than `UIViewController`.

Change this line at the top of the file from

```
class DetailViewController: UIViewController {
```

to the following:

```
class DetailViewController: UITableViewController {
```

Also change the storyboard so that the new `DetailViewController`'s type is `DetailViewController` (it might not be).

Remove references to the label from `DetailViewController` (it's called `DetailDescriptionLabel`).

There are a few housekeeping chores to tidy up the code. Change the variable declaration for detail to detailUser (at the top of the file).

Change detail to detailUser

```
var detailUser: User? {
  didSet {
    // Update the view.
    self.configureView
  }
}
```

Change configureCell to Use the Subclass

Here is what configureCell should look like now that it uses the Score subclass. Note that there's a bit of conversion going on as the NSSet of scores for a given user (a relationship) is converted to an array (so that the nth element can be found for the table). Then, the nth element (which is a Score) is examined to find its score value (Score.score).

```
func configureCell(cell: UITableViewCell, atIndexPath indexPath:
NSIndexPath) {
  if let scores = detailUser?.scores {
    let scoresArray = scores.allObjects as NSArray
    let selectedRowArrayElement = scoresArray [indexPath.row] as! Score
    let scoreForSelectedRow = selectedRowArrayElement.score
    cell.textLabel!.text = "Score: " + scoreForSelectedRow.description
  }
}
```

Modify MasterViewController to Pass the User to DetailViewController

By default, the object selected in the master detail view list is passed to DetailItem in DetailViewController. It's declared as AnyObject? You'll need to change it to use the new detailUser variable you've created. In prepareForSegue, change the line

```
controller.detailItem = object
```

to the following:

```
controller.detailUser = (object as! User)
```

You now need to connect the table and support the relevant protocols. This code is actually in MasterViewController because you need to manage a table view controller there. You'll just need to copy it to DetailViewController.

And you'll need to import Core Data at the top of `DetailViewController`.

```
import CoreData
```

Summary

You now have the basics of an app that uses the built-in SQLite database, the Xcode Core Data model editor and Core Data framework to work with the database, and the Cocoa Touch framework for iOS to bring it all together.

What you've seen in working with PHP and Core Data and in the summary of Android is that there are languages (PHP and others) as well as frameworks (Cocoa Touch and Cocoa) and application programming interfaces (APIs) (Android) that build on SQLite. The degree to which the SQL syntax for SQLite is exposed varies from very little (Core Data) to a great deal (PHP) and various middle roads such as Android.

What is important is that you understand the principles and functionality. Remember, too, that in building any database-driven app, the more that you can put into your database the less code you have to write. Take advantage of validation options, GROUP BY clauses, and everything else that you can find. The less code you write the less time it will take (to write and to debug!).

Index

■ X, Y, Z

Get the eBook for only $5!

Why limit yourself?

Now you can take the weightless companion with you wherever you go and access your content on your PC, phone, tablet, or reader.

Since you've purchased this print book, we're happy to offer you the eBook in all 3 formats for just $5.

Convenient and fully searchable, the PDF version enables you to easily find and copy code—or perform examples by quickly toggling between instructions and applications. The MOBI format is ideal for your Kindle, while the ePUB can be utilized on a variety of mobile devices.

To learn more, go to www.apress.com/companion or contact support@apress.com.

Printed in the United States
by Bookmasters

Printed in the United States
By Bookmasters